Living on Your Own

Second Edition

Jean Bunnell

User's Guide to Walch Reproducible Books

As part of our general effort to provide educational materials that are as practical and economical as possible, we have designated this publication a "reproducible book." The designation means that purchase of the book includes purchase of the right to limited reproduction of all pages on which this symbol appears:

Here is the basic Walch policy: We grant to individual purchasers of this book the right to make sufficient copies of reproducible pages for use by all students of a single teacher. This permission is limited to a single teacher and does not apply to entire schools or school systems, so institutions purchasing the book should pass the permission on to a single teacher. Copying of the book or its parts for resale is prohibited.

As noted in the text of this book, Walch also grants to purchasers the right to make transparency copies of certain sample pages for classroom overhead projection.

Any questions regarding this policy or requests to purchase further reproduction rights should be addressed to:

Permissions Editor
J. Weston Walch, Publisher
321 Valley Street • P.O. Box 658
Portland, Maine 04104-0658

About the Reading Level of Student Material

The authors and editors of *Living on Your Own* have made its basic text accessible to students with grade 3 and higher reading skills. But the program also includes realistic material that is unavoidably more demanding, and its use with some classes will require careful guidance and pre-teaching of vocabulary.

1 2 3 4 5 6 7 8 9 10

ISBN 0-8251-4281-4

J. Weston Walch, Publisher
P.O. Box 658 • Portland, Maine 04104-0658
www.walch.com

Printed in the United States of America

Contents

[* *All italicized material also appear in the workbook.*]

Part 4: Traveling in Rivertown and Walchville

Part 5: Choosing a Place to Live

Part 6: Adding Up the Costs

Part 7: Shopping for Food

Part 8: Cleaning Up

Part 9: Charging to the Future

Part 10: Continuing On

Rationale and Summary

Living on Your Own: An Independent Living Simulation offers classroom teachers a way to help students experience life in the real world. This teacher book and the accompanying student workbook provide all the materials you need for a simulation to help students develop essential life-management skills.

Divided into ten parts, this unit guides students step-by-step to assume responsibilities they will face once they are actually living on their own.

Students explore concepts consecutively and integrate what they learn into the expanding simulation experience. They begin by getting acquainted with the imaginary towns of Rivertown and Walchville. Then they find jobs, learn about the public transportation system, and consider their housing preferences. After searching the classified ads for an apartment, students deal with the realities of paying for utilities, shopping for food, and keeping their apartments clean. They make out a budget and learn to manage their money—cash, checking and savings accounts, and a charge account.

The *Living on Your Own* simulation spans twelve weeks, but these are imaginary weeks, and the activities can be done at whatever rate is comfortable for your students. Many activities are included to help your students learn about a variety of topics: how to live with a roommate; how to prepare a shopping list; how to make choices about which cleaning product to use; and much more.

Complete lesson plans, detailing ways to use this material with your class, accompany each part. In addition, information is included that suggests how you can personalize this simulation, using classified ads, maps, and public transportation schedules for your own community.

About This Edition

This 2001 version of *Living on Your Own* adds some new and helpful elements to what was already a widely used and highly successful program. Included are new activities in the parts on banking and housing, as well as new pre-teaching, evaluation, and extension activities for all parts. The revision also offers updated prices and other information throughout, and sports a new and simplified design.

Overview

Part Number and Activity Emphasis	Week of Simulation	New to Simulation	Continuing in Simulation
1. Introduction to the town	Preparation		
2. Getting a job	Week 1	Fill out time card for first week of work	
3. Savings account, checking account, and budget	Week 2	First paycheck Start checking account Start savings account	Fill out time card
4. Travel by bus	Week 3		Paycheck Checking account deposit Savings account deposit Fill out time card
5. Locate an apartment	Week 4	Write check for apartment deposit and first rent payment	Paycheck Checking account deposit Savings account deposit Fill out time card
6. Expenses	Week 5	Keep out money for out-of-pocket expenses Keep record of out-of-pocket expenses Pay utility deposits	Paycheck Checking account deposit Savings account deposit Pay rent by check if due weekly Fill out time card
7. Food	Week 6	Interest on savings account	Paycheck Checking account deposit Savings account deposit Keep out money for out-of-pocket expenses and keep track of how spent Pay rent by check if due weekly Write checks as needed Fill out time card

Overview *(continued)*

Part Number and Activity Emphasis	Week of Simulation	New to Simulation	Continuing in Simulation
8. Housecleaning	Week 7		Paycheck Checking account deposit Savings account deposit Keep out money for out-of-pocket expenses and keep track of how spent Pay rent by check if due weekly Write checks as needed Fill out time card
9. Charge cards	Week 8	Chance to charge larger purchases	Paycheck Checking account deposit Savings account deposit Keep out money for out-of-pocket expenses and keep track of how spent Pay rent by check if due weekly Write checks as needed Fill out time card
10. Continue the simulation	Week 9	Ups and downs of life	Paycheck Checking account deposit Savings account deposit Keep out money for out-of-pocket expenses and keep track of how spent Chance to charge larger purchases Pay rent by check if due weekly Pay rent by check if due monthly Write checks as needed Fill out time card

Overview *(continued)*

Part Number and Activity Emphasis	Week of Simulation	New to Simulation	Continuing in Simulation
	Week 10	Pay utility bills (electricity, gas, and phone)	Paycheck Checking account deposit Interest on savings account Savings account deposit Keep out money for out-of-pocket expenses and keep track of how spent Chance to charge larger purchases Pay rent by check if due weekly Write checks as needed Ups and downs of life Fill out time card
	Week 11	Charge payment due	Paycheck Checking account deposit Savings account deposit Keep out money for out-of-pocket expenses and keep track of how spent Chance to charge larger purchases Pay rent by check if due weekly Write checks as needed Ups and downs of life Fill out time card
	Week 12	Add interest to charge account statement	Paycheck Checking account deposit Savings account deposit Keep out money for out-of-pocket expenses and keep track of how spent Chance to charge larger purchases Pay rent by check if due weekly Write checks as needed Ups and downs of life Fill out time card

Some Simulation Options

Living on Your Own can be used in a variety of ways, depending on the needs and abilities of your students. Consider the following possibilities.

1. Do the simulation as written, with each student finding a job, locating a place to live, and dealing with everyday life in Rivertown and Walchville.
2. Adapt the simulation to your own town. Use a map of your community, hometown newspaper ads for jobs and apartments, and local public transportation schedules.
3. Have your class work as a whole or in small groups to complete the simulation. The class or each small group can collectively become a person who finds a job, takes an apartment, and lives independently.
4. Do one part each week. Set aside a specific day or days for several weeks to work on the simulation. Continue with other classroom activities on the remaining days each week.
5. Use the unit on a continuing instead of a weekly basis, going directly from Part 1 to Part 2, etc. More advanced students will be able to do some parts in a day or two. Others may require up to a week for the same work.
6. Choose only some parts to do with your class. For example, you might skip Parts 1 and 3, starting with Part 2 and continuing with Part 4. Or you might conclude with Part 8.

Adapting This Simulation to Your Own Community

You don't need to move your students to Rivertown and Walchville. You can adapt this simulation to your own community instead. This chart tells you how.

Part	What You Need	Directions
1	Maps and street directories for your city or town	Follow the general lesson plan in the teacher book, substituting maps and street directories for your own city or town. Other suggestions: (a) Make observations about special features of city or town. (b) Talk about scale of miles. (c) Use street directory to locate places. (d) On the board, list several places, such as the bus station, the library, hospitals, etc. Give streets where each is located and have students locate on map.
2	Help-wanted ads in the classified section of your own newspaper Activities 2, 3, 4, 5	Follow the general lesson plan in the teacher book, substituting your own classified ads. For each job listed, you will need job descriptions (such as the ones for Rivertown and Walchville on pages 24–32 of the teacher book). Information on job descriptions will need to include: (a) Employer (b) Location (c) Job (d) Skills needed (e) Hours (f) Benefits (g) Wages (h) Take-home pay
3		As written

Adapting This Simulation to Your Own Community *(continued)*

Part	What You Need	Directions
4	Public transportation maps and schedules for your city or town Activity 11 Questions 1–7 can be used; substitute appropriate questions for 8–10	Follow the general lesson plan in the teacher book, substituting your own public transportation maps and schedules. Discuss: (a) Where routes go (b) How to read timetable
5	Apartment-rental ads in the classified section of your own newspaper Activities 13, 14, 15, 16	Follow the general lesson plan in the teacher book, substituting your own classified ads. For each apartment students "rent," they will need to know: (a) Location of apartment (b) Landlord's name (c) Rent (monthly or weekly) (d) Utilities they will have to pay (e) Cost of first month's service for utilities they need to pay
6		You may choose to have students make out utility deposits to your own local electric, gas, or phone company.
7		As written
8		As written
9		As written
10		As in Part 6, you may choose to have students pay local utilities.

Further Suggestions

Most of the workbook answer pages reproduced in the teacher book have been completed by a fictitious student, Lee West. This is to help you and your class see how one student might do the pages. If you have the facilities available, it may be helpful for you to make transparencies of some of these pages for use with an overhead projector. Go over Lee's entries with your students so they can see how someone else dealt with the problems they will face.

Pencil may be the best writing tool for students to use on the activity pages in their workbooks. Pen is fine for some activities, but students will have figuring to do on many pages and may want to make corrections or changes.

This is only a simulation. Class members can control some choices as it progresses, but they will encounter some unexpected expenses through the random selection of events in later parts. One or two students may become upset if their expenses grow larger than they can afford. Remind them that this is not real life, and nobody is playing for keeps. The point is for students to learn from this simulation so they can prepare for actually living on their own—when they sometimes will have unexpected problems and expenses.

Use your own common sense and creativity and encourage your students to do the same. Life is not correct or incorrect. Every effort has been made to address problems that may confront you and your students during this simulation, but there is always something new. Even if a situation has been considered in the teacher book, you may not be able to put your finger on the information right when you want it. So . . . do what makes sense to you.

Use your own judgment, too, in dealing with disparities between information provided by the book and what you find in your own area. You may discover, for example, that pay rates and housing costs seem wrong for your area. Such items vary considerably from one community to the next, and there is no way that a simulation like *Living on Your Own* can reflect the true situation in every area. You should probably alert your students to any disparity you find, but also point out that the concepts and processes taught by the simulation remain valid everywhere. See also "Adapting This Simulation to Your Own Community," beginning on page *xiii*.

There is no right or wrong way to conduct this simulation. Every situation is different. Adapt these materials and use them in the way that will work best in your classroom.

Using the Lesson Plans

A detailed lesson plan is included for each part of this simulation. Here's what you get for all ten parts:

Objectives: Clear statements tell what the students will accomplish in each part. Objectives are specific in listing for you and the students what they will be learning.

Materials Needed: A short list tells what you will need for each part. Items include activities in the student workbook, pencils, rulers, and any simulation materials the teacher will need to copy before class. When preparing these paper materials, consider making transparency versions or enlarged copies to display.

Pre-teaching: Student readiness for this simulation will vary. The lesson plan mentions concepts and vocabulary you might wish to review with your class before introducing a lesson.

Introduction: A suggestion for introducing each lesson is included. Each introduction is written as commentary, in the actual words that a teacher can use in presenting the material to students. When the commentary includes questions to ask students, the answers to the questions are given in italic type.

Activities: Copies of all activity pages are part of the teacher book at the end of each lesson plan. The lesson plan lists the number for the activity being done. With each activity, there is specific commentary that teachers may find helpful to follow when reviewing it with students.

Activity Answers: Answers for the activity pages are written on the activity pages in the teacher book. For the end-of-week activities, "Living on Your Own," sample answers have been given by "Lee West." These sample answers will help address any questions about how students should complete the activity pages.

Simulation Materials: Job and apartment descriptions, utility bills, and the "ups and downs of life" are some of the simulation materials teachers will need to copy from the teacher book for use with the students. All materials and specific directions are included in the lesson plans.

Evaluation: Reviewing completed activity pages and asking review questions can help you evaluate the success of each lesson. Some of these questions can help students apply what they are learning in Rivertown and Walchville to their own real communities.

Extension Activities: You may wish to build on *Living on Your Own* by giving your class additional activities that will expand their understanding and help them apply what they learn to their own communities. The lesson plans provide a wide range of ideas.

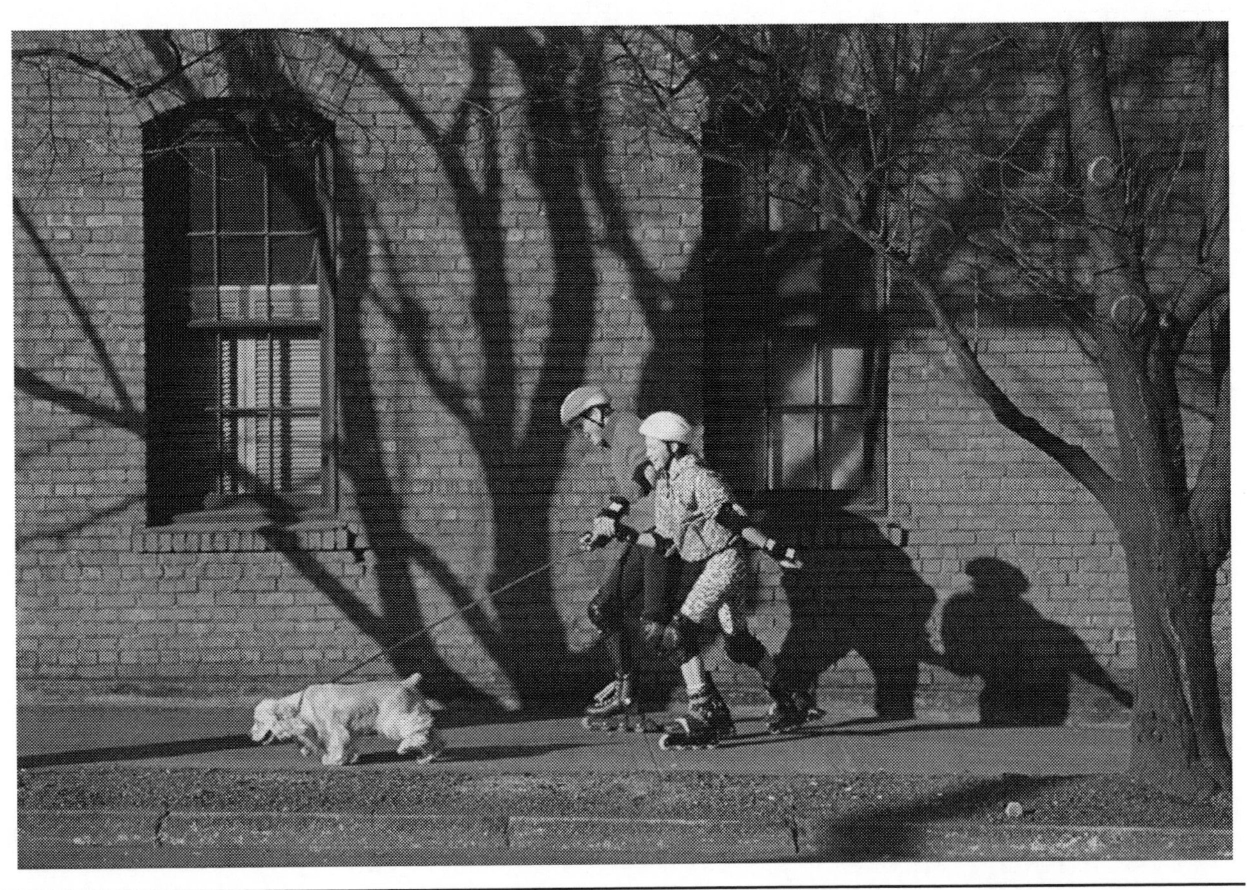

Part 1: Getting to Know Rivertown and Walchville

Part 1: Getting to Know Rivertown and Walchville

Objectives

- Students will learn to use a scale of miles and the street directory to find places on a map.
- Students will get acquainted with the imaginary towns of Rivertown and Walchville.

Materials Needed

Maps (workbook, pages 4 and 5; teacher book, pages 6 and 7); (**Note:** Map in student workbook shows only streets. Parks, buildings, etc. are shown in the teacher book. Activity 1: Find Your Way Around Town requires students to locate and mark these areas.)

Street directory (workbook, page 6; teacher book, page 8)

Activity 1: Find Your Way Around Town

Pencils

Rulers

Pre-teaching

Be sure students are comfortable with the names of the four directions—*north*, *south*, *east*, and *west*—and with their combinations—*northeast*, *southeast*, *southwest*, and *northwest*. Review any workbook vocabulary you think may challenge your class. Consider these terms: *bordered by* and *intersection*.

Commentary: Introduction

For the next few weeks, we are going to pretend we are living and working in the imaginary towns of Rivertown and Walchville. Everyone will be finding a job, locating a place to live, and doing the things that are part of everyday life.

Commentary: Map

Look at the map of Rivertown and Walchville.

What do you notice about the two towns?

Walch River divides the two towns.

Rivertown is to the west of the river.

Walchville is to the east of the river.

Piers extend into the river.

The streets of Rivertown are close together near the river and more spread out farther away.

How do you know which direction is which?

The north arrow next to the scale of miles points up. So south is down, west is left, and east is right.

Commentary: Scale

Notice the scale of miles in the lower left corner of the map. Use your ruler to find how many inches on the map equal a mile.

There should be 2 inches to a mile.

If something measures 1 inch, how many miles is it?

$^1/_2$ *mile*

What if something is 5 inches?

$2^1/_2$ *miles*

Measure the part of the Walch River that is shown on the map. How long is it?

9 inches

So how many miles of the river are shown on the map?

$4^1/_2$ *miles*

Note: Consider expanding this practice if your class seems confused about using the scale of miles.

Commentary: Street Directory

Notice the numbers and letters around the map. They help in locating streets on the map.

Ohio street is located at B1. Find B on the top or bottom of the map. Find 1 on the side of the map. Ohio Street is where these two come together.

Try finding Woodfords Street, which stretches from E5 to G4.

The directory on page 6 lists all the streets in Rivertown and Walchville.

Look at Orange Street. What information will help us locate it on the map?

F6–F7

How about Boyd Street? That is not listed under streets in Rivertown. So look in Walchville. It is J4–J5. Find Boyd Street on your map.

Commentary: Worksheet 1: Find Your Way Around Town

Cities usually have hospitals, parks, schools, shopping centers, a bus station, city hall, and entertainment areas. This activity page tells the street where each of these places is located in Rivertown and Walchville. Use the street directory to find where the streets are on the map. Find the location of each place and write it on the map. Most places are identified as being at the intersection of two or more streets. There are no street numbers.

Let's do the first one together. Central Park is in Rivertown and is bordered by Brackett Street, Spring Street, Pine Street, and Deering Avenue. Find each of these streets.

Brackett Street F2–H3

Spring Street F3–I1

Pine Street E3–F2

Deering Avenue F1–F4

Activity Answers

Places have been shown on the map in the teacher book on pages 6 and 7.

Evaluation

Check student progress and understanding by reviewing completed workbook pages. Ask questions like these, using some to help students understand how they can apply their developing skills to their own communities:

- If you lived next to the bus station, what letter and number would you use to describe the location?
- What direction would you go to get from the health center in Walchville to the Civic Center in Rivertown?
- Does the map of Walchville look like our town? What are some of the differences? What about Rivertown?
- Do you think you could draw a map of our town if you had enough time? What would some of the problems be?

Extension Activities

Obtain maps of your own community and share them with students. Explain any distance and directional symbols. Help students find such places as their schools, their residences, prominent public buildings, and major places of employment.

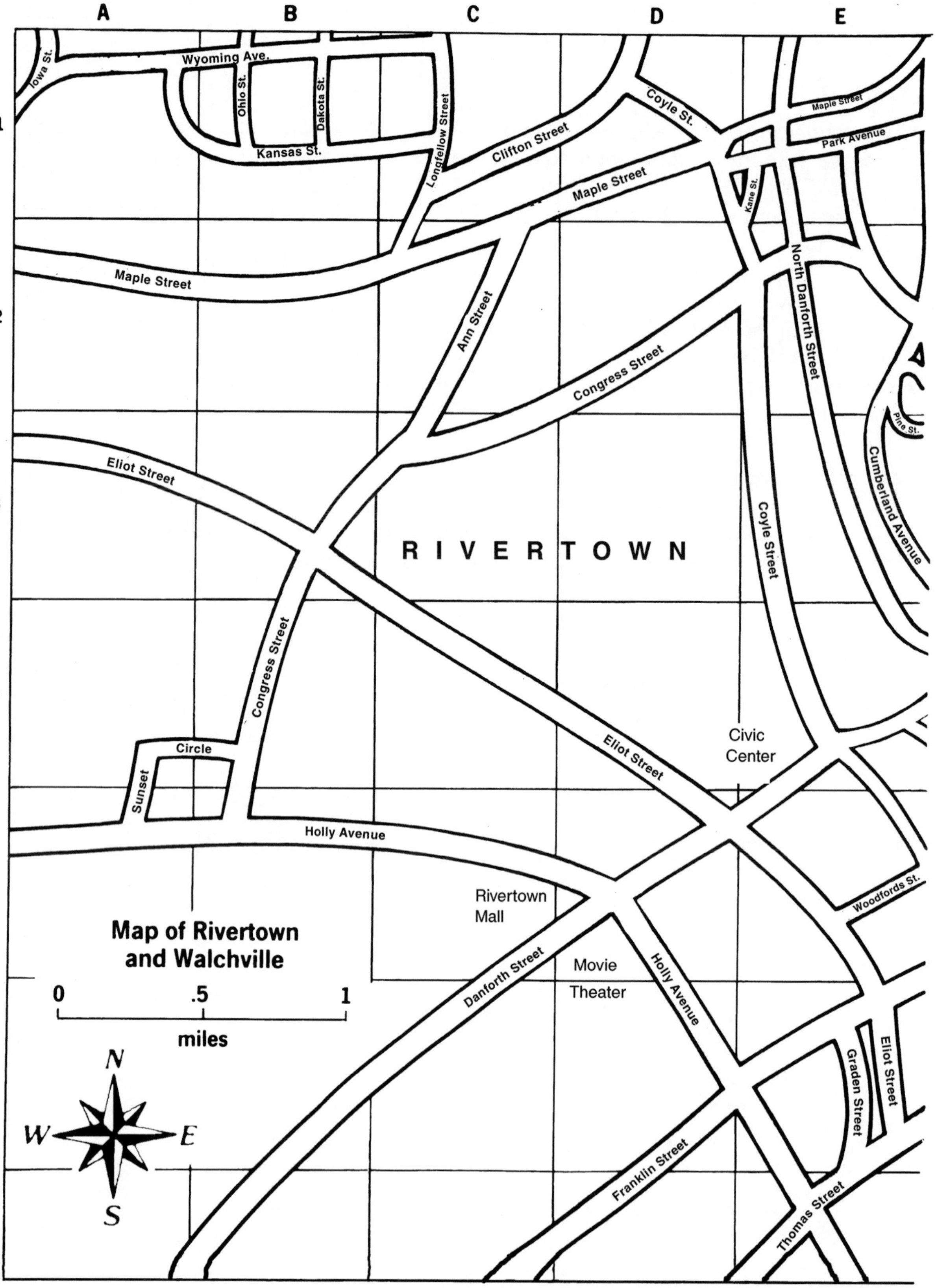

A B C D E

1 2 3 4 5 6 7

Iowa St.
Wyoming Ave.
Ohio St.
Dakota St.
Kansas St.
Longfellow Street
Clifton Street
Coyle St.
Maple Street
Park Avenue
Maple Street
Kane St.
Maple Street
Ann Street
Congress Street
North Danforth Street
Pine St.
Cumberland Avenue
Eliot Street
RIVERTOWN
Coyle Street
Congress Street
Civic Center
Eliot Street
Circle
Sunset
Holly Avenue
Rivertown Mall
Woodfords St.
Movie Theater
Danforth Street
Holly Avenue
Graden Street
Eliot Street
Franklin Street
Thomas Street

Map of Rivertown and Walchville

0 .5 1

miles

N
W E
S

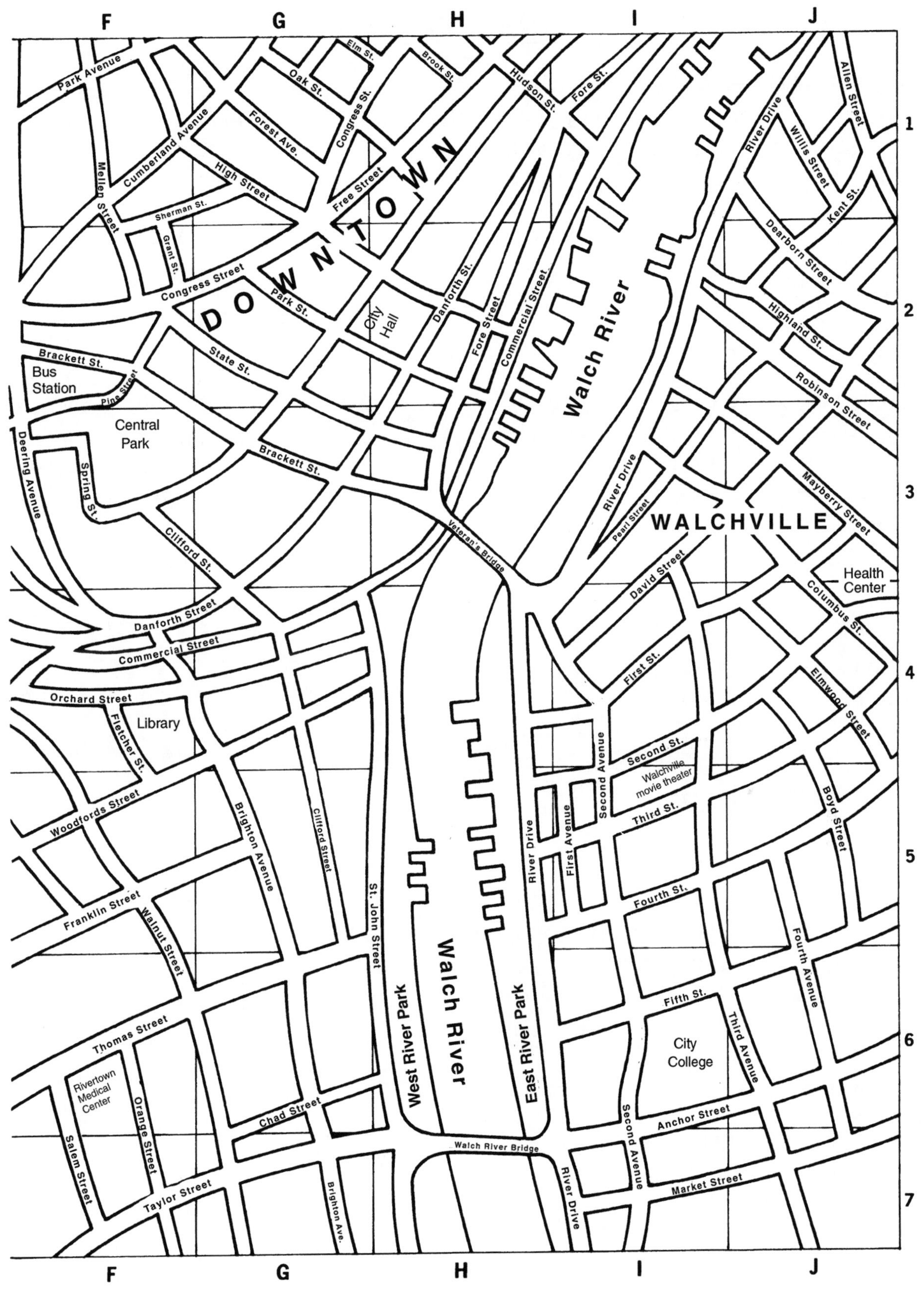
F
G
H
I
J
1
2
3
4
5
6
7
DOWNTOWN
WALCHVILLE
Walch River
Walch River
Park Avenue
Elm St.
Brook St.
Hudson St.
Fore St.
Oak St.
Congress St.
Forest Ave.
Cumberland Avenue
High Street
Free Street
Mellen Street
Sherman St.
Grant St.
Congress Street
Park St.
City Hall
Danforth St.
Fore Street
Commercial Street
State St.
Brackett St.
Bus Station
Pine Street
Central Park
Deering Avenue
Spring St.
Brackett St.
Clifford St.
Veteran's Bridge
Danforth Street
Commercial Street
Orchard Street
Fletcher St.
Library
Woodfords Street
Brighton Avenue
Clifford Street
St. John Street
Franklin Street
Walnut Street
Thomas Street
Rivertown Medical Center
Orange Street
Salem Street
Chad Street
Taylor Street
Brighton Ave.
West River Park
East River Park
Walch River Bridge
River Drive
Allen Street
Willis Street
Kent St.
River Drive
Dearborn Street
Highland St.
Robinson Street
River Drive
Pearl Street
Mayberry Street
Health Center
David Street
Columbus St.
First St.
Elmwood Street
Second St.
Walchville movie theater
Second Avenue
Third St.
First Avenue
River Drive
Boyd Street
Fourth St.
Fourth Avenue
Fifth St.
Third Avenue
City College
Anchor Street
Second Avenue
Market Street
River Drive
F
G
H
I
J

Street Directory

Streets of Rivertown

Street	Location
Ann St.	C2
Brackett St.	F2–H3
Brighton Ave.	F4–G7
Brook St.	H1
Chad St.	G6
Clifford St.	F3–G5
Clifton St.	C1–D1
Commercial St.	F4–I1
Congress St.	B5–H1
Coyle St.	D1–F5
Cumberland Ave.	E3–G1
Dakota St.	B1
Danforth St.	A7–H1
Deering Ave.	F1–F4
Eliot St.	A3–E6
Elm St.	G1–H1
Fletcher St.	F4–F5
Fore St.	H3–I1
Forest Ave.	G1
Franklin St.	C7–G5
Free St.	G1–H1
Graden St.	E6
Grant St.	F2
High St.	F1–H2
Holly Ave.	A5–E7
Hudson St.	H1–I1
Iowa St.	A1
Kane St.	E1
Kansas St.	A1–C1
Longfellow St.	C1–C2
Maple St.	A2–E1
Mellen St.	F1–F2
North Danforth St.	E1–F4
Oak St.	G1–H1
Ohio St.	B1
Orange St.	F6–F7
Orchard St.	F4–G4
Park Ave.	D1–F1
Park St.	G2–H2
Pine St.	E3–F2
Salem St.	F6–F7
Sherman St.	F1–G1
Spring St.	F3–I1
St. John St.	G4–H7
State St.	F2–H3
Sunset Circle	A5–B4
Taylor St.	F7–H7
Thomas St.	E7–G6
Walnut St.	E4–G7
Woodfords St.	E5–G4
Wyoming Ave.	A1–C1

Streets of Walchville

Street	Location
Allen St.	J1
Anchor St.	I6–J6
Boyd St.	J4–J5
Columbus St.	I3–J4
David St.	I4–J2
Dearborn St.	J1–J2
Elmwood St.	J4
Fifth St.	I6–J5
First Ave.	I5
First St.	H4–J3
Fourth Ave.	J5–J7
Fourth St.	H5–J4
Highland St.	I2–J3
Kent St.	J1–J2
Market St.	I7–J6
Mayberry St.	I2–J3
Pearl St.	I3–J2
River Drive	I7–J1
Robinson St.	I2–J3
Second Ave.	H4–I7
Second St.	H5–J4
Third Ave.	I3–J7
Third St.	H5–J4
Willis St.	J1

Student page 7

1. Find Your Way Around Town

Use the maps on pages 4 and 5 to locate some of the public buildings and areas in Rivertown and Walchville. Rivertown is west of the Walch River. Walchville is east of the river. Write the name of each building or area where you find it on the map.

Parks

- Central Park (Rivertown)
  Block bordered by Brackett Street, Spring Street, Pine Street, and Deering Avenue
- West River Park (Rivertown)
  Between St. John Street and Walch River
- East River Park (Walchville)
  South of Veteran's Bridge between River Drive and Walch River

Medical Treatment Facilities

- Rivertown Medical Center
  Thomas Street between Orange Street and Salem Street
- Health Center (Walchville)
  South of the intersection of Mayberry Street and First Street

Shopping Centers

- Downtown: Congress and Free Streets between State Street and Hudson Street
- Rivertown Mall: Southwest of the intersection of Holly Avenue and Danforth Street

Bus Station

- Across from Central Park at intersection of Pine Street and Deering Avenue

Civic Center

- Danforth Street between Coyle Street and Eliot Street

Movie Theaters

- Rivertown: Danforth Street across from the mall
- Walchville: South side of Second Street, at corner of Third Avenue

City Hall

- Southeast side of Spring Street between Park Street and High Street

City College

- Block bordered by Fifth Street, Third Avenue, Anchor Street, and Second Avenue in Walchville

Library

- Rivertown: Orchard Street between Fletcher Street and Brighton Avenue

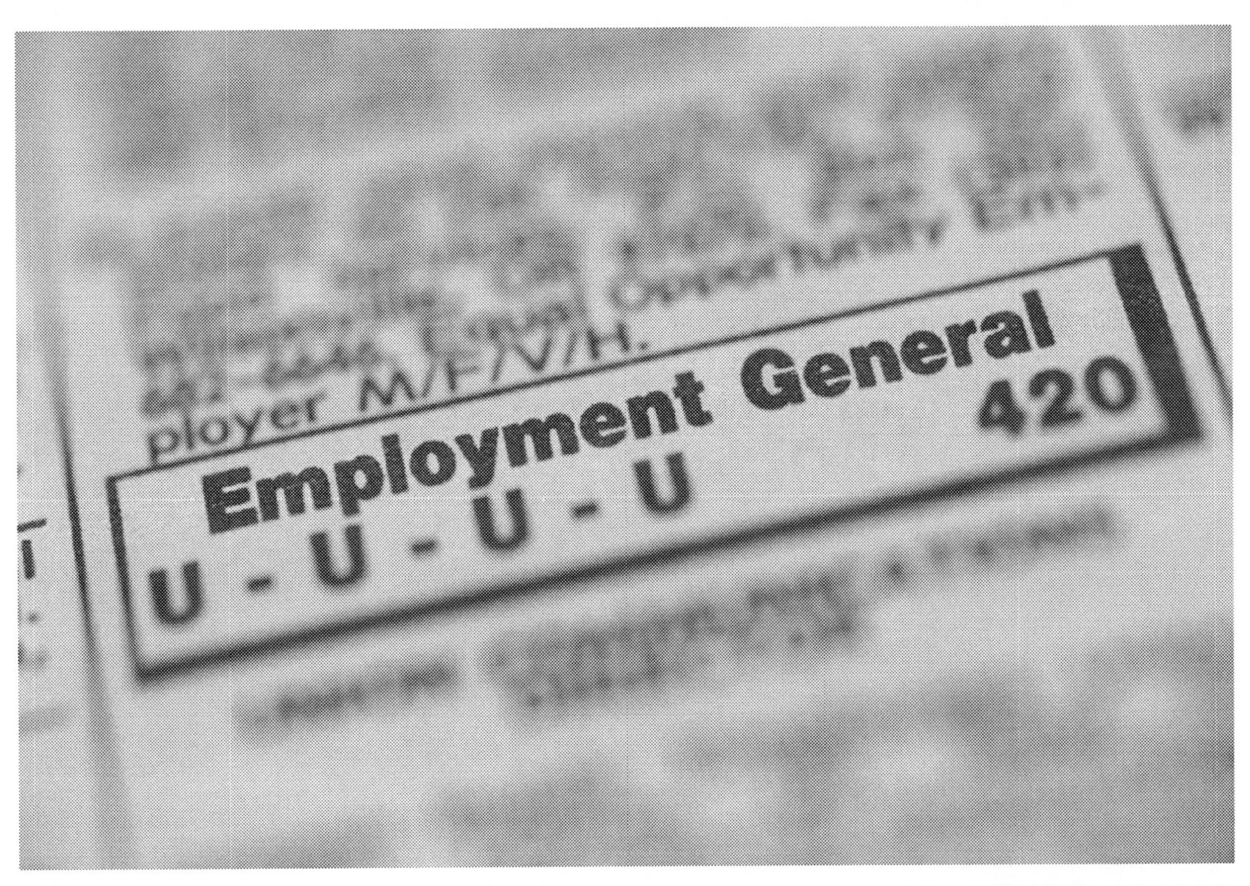

Part 2:
Getting a Good Job

Part 2: Getting a Good Job

Objectives

- Students will identify what they want in jobs.
- Students will use the classified ads from a newspaper to search for jobs.
- Students will select the jobs they will have for this simulation.
- Students will complete the first week of the simulation.

Materials Needed

Activity 2: The Right Job for You

Classified Ads (workbook pages 11 and 12; teacher book pages 21 and 22)

Activity 3: Job Hunting in the Classifieds

Explanations of Job Descriptions (teacher book page 23)

Copies of Job Descriptions (teacher book pages 24–32)

Tape for attaching job descriptions to workbooks

Activity 4: Application for Employment

Activity 5: Week 1—Living on Your Own

Pre-teaching

Be sure students understand these words related to the general topic of finding jobs: *application, benefit, classified ads, employee, employment, skills,* and *talents.*

Review vocabulary associated with the classified ads either before using them or while going through them with the class. Difficult words include (in order of their appearance): *technician, clerical, word processing, order entry, group insurance, preferred, dietary, flexible, facility, reconditioning, placement, awnings, experience, maintenance, administration, attendant, custom, receptionist, entry level, competitive, retail, motivated, stockroom, deliveries, terminal, training, uniforms, profit sharing, utility, errands, switchboard, assemblers, factory, ambitious, progressive, electronics, candidates, wafer, fabrication, merit pay, modern, paneling, manufacturing,* and *willingness.*

Review vocabulary associated with the application for employment either before using it or while reviewing it with the class. Difficult words include: *personal, Social Security, permanent, commercial, inquire, availability, indicate, qualifications, possess, licenses, certifications, former, responsibilities, prospective, consideration, discrimination, creed, national origin, imply, warrant, certify, falsified, statements, grounds for dismissal, authorize, investigation, herein, references, pertinent parties, liability, furnishing, definite, regardless, terminated,* and *prior notice.*

Commentary: Introduction

What's the first thing you need if you are going to live on your own?

Income; money

For that, you will need a job.

To start the process of job hunting, you will need to think about what skills you have and what you want to do for work. Everybody has strengths that make them good at some jobs. You need to know what yours are. You also need to think about your own needs. How much money do you need to make? What hours can you work? Once you know those things, you can look through the classifieds to find the jobs you want to apply for. When you have a job, you will need to fill out a time card so you can get paid and start living on your own.

Commentary: Activity 2: The Right Job for You

Thinking about the questions in this activity will help you decide what kind of job would be best for you.

For question 8, blank lines have been included so that you can add other skills you may be able to offer an employer.

If you need more room to answer questions 9 and 10, use another piece of paper.

Note: Review this page with students at the level needed for them to use it successfully.

Commentary: Classified Ads

Look at the help wanted ads on pages 11 and 12. They include a wide variety of jobs, and each ad gives a little different information. The first ad, in fact, is advertising for two jobs. What are they?

Prep cook; P.M. dishwasher

Who is advertising for help?

LoMein Restaurant on Chad Street

Can you call for more information?

The ad says "No phone calls."

What other information is given in the ad?

Apply 10:30–11:30 A.M. or after 2 P.M.

Look at the next ad, for an automotive technician. What information is given that was not in the first ad?

Phone number; starting pay

Look at the next one—a large ad wanting clerical help. It tells about a benefits package. What does that include?

Paid holidays, vacations, group insurance

Note: You and the class might read through the ads together to ensure that everyone understands what each job is. Students can take turns reading the ads aloud. Talk about what each job might entail, and assist with vocabulary as necessary.

Commentary: Activity 3: Job Hunting in the Classifieds

As you complete this activity, you will be reading through these ads and comparing different jobs. Remembering what you learned about yourself from Activity 2: The Right Job for You, select three jobs that you might like to apply for.

Job Students Want to Apply For

Note: In the teacher book, each ad is identified with a number. Ads for two jobs (such as the first ad placed by LoMein Restaurant) have two numbers. The numbers will help you easily match the ads with the job descriptions given on pages 24–32 of the teacher book. An explanation of the information included in the job descriptions is given on page 23 of the teacher book.

On the chart below, write the names of the students interested in each job.
Note: * indicates that the ad lists a phone number to call for more information.

Job		Interested Students
1.	Prep Cook	
2.	Dishwasher	
3.	*Automotive Technician	
4.	*Auto Reconditioning	
5.	*Clerical	
6.	Dietary Aide	
7.	Prep Cook	
8.	Maid	
9.	*Awning Technician	
10.	*Baker's Assistant	
11.	Bottle Sorter	
12.	*Carpenter's Helper	
13.	Custodian	
14.	*Cleaning	
15.	*Counter Person	
16.	Dietary Aide	
17.	*Gas Station Attendant	
18.	*Laundry Helper	
19.	Lawn Spraying	
20.	*Cleaning	
21.	*Day Care Person	
22.	*Office Delivery	
23.	*Painter	
24.	Receptionist	
25.	Sales Help	
26.	*Carpet Installer	
27.	*Service Station Attendant	
28.	Stockroom/Delivery	
29.	*Terminal Workers	

30.	Room Attendant	
31.	Housekeeper	
32.	Truck Loading	
33.	*Utility Clerk/Driver	
34.	*Window Assembler	
35.	Production Worker	
36.	Panel Manufacture	

Note: At this point, teachers can simply assign jobs to all students, have them fill out the application, give them a copy of the job description, and proceed with Activity 5: Week 1—Living on Your Own.

As an alternative, teachers can involve the students in a role play. Specific role-play guidelines are given below.

Commentary: Calling for More Information

Note: Job ads that list a phone number to call for information are marked with an * in the chart above. Select several of these jobs that students have shown interest in.

Now let's talk about actually applying for a job. When a job ad lists a phone number, you can call to get more information about the job or to arrange an interview. We're going to role-play calling for more information.

One student will read the ad and then call for more details. Someone else will have a copy of the job description for that job and pretend to be the employer who answers the phone when the student calls.

Before making a call, you will want to have several questions in mind to ask the potential employer. In real life, you always want to be truthful when talking to a potential employer. This is a little different because we are imagining what life will be like when you are through school and on your own. In these role plays, it is okay to add extra information or give details about yourself that aren't correct (for example, you can say that you have finished high school even if you are only a sophomore).

Note: For the first role play, it may be helpful if the teacher takes the role of the employer answering the phone. Use the job description to help you answer questions and ask questions of the student. The student wanting more information about a job will place the call and initiate the conversation.

For example, a student is interested in working at a day care center (Job 21).

Student: Calling 748-1198

Employer: Hello. Walchville Day Care Center.

Student: My name is ________. I saw your ad in the paper and I am interested in learning more about the job.

Employer: We are a day care center licensed to care for up to thirty pre-school children. The children range from one to five years old. There are two teachers and three assistants. The opening is for an assistant.

Student: What does the job involve?

Employer: You will be working directly with the children and also preparing breakfast and lunch for them. The hours are from 7 A.M. to 4 P.M.

Student: I baby-sit quite a bit and like to be with little kids.

Employer: How are your cooking skills?

Student: I can't make anything fancy, but I'm sure I will be able to fix cereal or sandwiches.

Employer: How much education have you had?

Student: I will be graduating from high school in two months. We studied child care in home economics, and this is the kind of job I would like to get.

Employer: The pay is $7.00 an hour. And employees get health insurance as well as paid holidays. Are you still interested?

Student: Yes.

Employer: Then I'd like to have you come for an interview. How about next Tuesday at 3:00?

Student: That would be fine. Where are you located?

Employer: At the corner of Third Avenue and First Street in Walchville. When you come, please bring two letters of reference. Perhaps you could get a letter from your home economics teacher and a letter from the people you baby-sit for.

Student: I can do that. See you next Tuesday.

Employer: I look forward to meeting you. Good-bye.

Note: For some calls, have an answering machine respond so students can see how they would handle that situation.

Commentary: A Job

Some ads ask potential employees to apply in person. We're going to role-play applying in person.

Before applying, you will want to think about what you expect will happen and be ready to talk with someone about the qualifications you have and why you want the job.

In doing these role plays, it is okay to add extra information or give details about yourself that aren't correct (for example, you can say that you have a driver's license even if you don't).

Note: For the first role play, it may be helpful if the teacher takes the role of the employer talking with the potential employee. Use the job description to help you answer questions and ask questions of the student. The student applying for the job will enter and initiate the conversation.

For example, a student is interested in working as a stockroom/delivery person for a printer (Job 28).

Student: Is this where I apply for the job advertised in the paper?

Employer: What job is that?

Student: The paper said that Friendly Printer is looking for someone to work in the stockroom and to make deliveries.

Employer: This is the place. Are you interested in the job?

Student: Yes, I am.

Employer: Do you have a driver's license?

Student: Yes.

Employer: How long have you been driving?

Student: Two years.

Employer: Ever had any accidents?

Student: No.

Employer: Any speeding convictions?

Student: None.

Employer: How long have you lived in the area?

Student: All my life, and I know the streets of Rivertown and Walchville very well.

Employer: Is that so? Well, you look strong enough to handle the lifting. How's your health?

Student: I'm hardly ever sick.

Employer: Why do you want the job?

Student: Because I like to be out and do a variety of things. I don't want to get stuck inside doing the same thing all day. With this job, I could be out meeting people.

Employer: I'll expect you to work hard, not be out chatting all day.

Student: I understand that.

Employer: Well, fill out this application. Be sure to include the phone numbers of at least two people I can call about you. I'll let you know by the first of next week.

Student: Thank you very much.

Commentary: Activity 4: Application for Employment

Most employers ask a prospective employee to fill out an application. Decide which job you most want and fill out Activity 4: Application for Employment.

Note: Discuss the form with the class before students fill it out. If you have made a transparency, use it for this process. Give some attention to the small print at the end of the form. Be sure that students understand its general purpose and meaning, even if they cannot define every word it contains. *(It says that the employer does not discriminate and that the employer can fire the worker at any time. The person signing it says that all his or her answers are true. If that's not the case, the person can be fired. The signer also gives the company permission to talk to references and earlier employers.)* Give attention to the former employer and references sections. For purposes of this simulation, dates and addresses don't have to be exact. But in real life, of course, accuracy is important. Point out that in real life, applicants should fill things out neatly and use a pen. There should be no cross-outs. Consider giving students a second copy of the form so they use the first as a draft and the second for a neat, final version. Be sure that students identify their desired employer and job title at the top of the form.

Commentary: Activity 5: Week 1—Living on Your Own

Note: Ahead of class, make a copy of the job description for the job each student has chosen. Cut job descriptions apart. For this simulation, it is fine for several students to select the same job.

This is the first week of actually "living" in Rivertown and Walchville. You will receive the job description for the job you have selected and use the information to fill out this activity page. But for just a minute, let's look at some of the vocabulary words on the page.

What does the word "employer" mean?

Person or company you work for

What is an "employee"?

Person hired to do the work

What is the "hourly rate of pay"?

Amount paid for each hour of work

What is the "weekly gross pay"?

Number of hours worked times hourly rate

What is "take-home pay"?

Amount you actually get after taxes and other deductions are subtracted from gross pay

What are "benefits"?

Things, such as health insurance and vacation, employee receives in addition to pay

What is a "time card"?

Record of number of hours worked

How do you count your hours?

Figure out how many hours you work each day, then add them up. Notice that some job descriptions say you get an unpaid hour or half hour for meals. You do not count those hours.

Finish the activity and fill in the time card for your first week of work.

Note: Some students without employment experience may be surprised at the difference between gross pay and take-home pay. Point out that the actual difference in real life depends on many things—your tax rate, for example, and your benefits. If your employer takes too much money out for taxes, you will get some back at the end of the year. If he or she doesn't take enough, you must pay more taxes at the end of the year. In this simulation, take-home pay is approximately 75 percent of gross pay. Therefore, the amount of money subtracted for missing an hour of work is also 75 percent of the hourly rate of pay.

Evaluation

Check student progress and understanding by reviewing completed workbook pages. Ask questions like these, using some to help students understand how they can apply their developing skills in their own lives:

- Would you really want the job you have taken for this class? Why or why not?

- What's one thing you have learned about applying for jobs?
- Have you had real employment interviews? What were they like?
- What should you do if you can't understand something on an application form? (*Ask for help. That's better than doing it wrong.*)
- Do you think you are ready to apply for a job? If your answer is "no," how can you get ready?

Extension Activities

Get application forms from local businesses for students to see. Or assign students to go to those businesses and get forms for the class to review. Talk about how to do this. (*In small businesses, talk to the person who seems to be in charge. In large businesses, ask the receptionist, or go to the human resources department or the personnel department. You can also telephone and ask for a form, but you won't get to see the business if you do that.*) You could copy some of those forms for additional class practice in filling them out. Point out that classified ads are only one way to find out about job openings, and ask the class to suggest others. (*Talking to friends or family members, watching school bulletin boards, going to an employment agency.*) Ask students what difficult questions employers might ask in interviews. (*Why should I hire you? Why did you leave an earlier job so soon? How good are your school grades? Are you sure you can lift heavy boxes all day?*) List some of those questions, and ask for possible answers. Or create role plays around them. Talk about preparing for a job interview. (*Dress correctly. Plan your answers to questions. Know what your strengths are. Don't chew gum. Be polite.*) Discuss common job benefits, like insurance, vacation time, and sick days. Point out that it can be difficult to find jobs with good benefits. Many employers today don't hire many full-time workers. They get part-time employees and do not give benefits. Talk about keeping a job once you have it. (*Know how to get along with others. Listen to directions. Read the rules in the employee handbook and follow them. Be on time—or early. Ask questions if you don't know what to do. Have a good attitude.*) Talk about handling problems with previous employment. (*Be honest and list the place where you worked. If an interviewer asks what happened, explain. If you were fired for a mistake you made, say how you have changed and why you won't repeat the mistake.*) Mention that students should ask permission from teachers and others before using them as references. (*Say, may I use you as a reference?*)

Classified Ads: Help Wanted

HELP WANTED

AM/PM Prep Cook, PM Dishwasher. Apply at LoMein Restaurant on Chad Street 10:30–11:30 A.M. or after 2 P.M. No phone calls. (1-2)

AUTO TECHNICIAN (3) to change oil filter and lube. Starting pay, $8 per hour. Go to Speedy Auto Care, 27 Sherman St. or call 293-4761.

(4) AUTO RECONDITIONING POSITION

Available immediately for placement on the night shift. Experience not required. Will train. Night shift hours 4:30 P.M. to 1 A.M. Contact Bud Smith 293-4288 for interview.

Rivertown Dodge

CLERICAL HELP (5)

For a growing firm. Duties include: word processing, order entry, filing and telephone use. Benefits include: paid holidays, vacations, and group insurance plan. Experience preferred but not required. Call Sandra for an appointment.

MILL CO.
102 Kent St.
Walchville
748-9032

DIETARY AIDES WANTED (6)

Full time, flexible hours. Every other weekend. Experience preferred. Must be 16-years-old. Apply at:

WALCHVILLE HEALTH CARE FACILITY
First Avenue, Walchville

JOIN OUR WINNING TEAM! OPENINGS FOR: (7-8)

* Prep Cooks
* Maids

AM and PM shifts. Apply in person between 8 and 11 A.M. or 2 and 5 P.M.

Martin's Inn
248 Clifton St., Rivertown

AWNING TECHNICIAN (9) Need immediately to install home and commercial awnings.
For appt. call
Leavitt Awning Company
293-2198

BAKER'S ASSISTANT (10) NEEDED—For daytime shift. Pay based on experience. Insurance, paid vacations, benefits, etc. Call for appointment 293-4110.

BOTTLE SORTERS—Full time needed $7.50/hour. Must work a varied schedule. Fill out an application at Rivertown Redemption Center, Maple & Longfellow St. (11)

CARPENTER'S HELPER. Will train. Must have own car. 347-9186 (12)

CIVIC CENTER— (13) CUSTODIAL/BUILDING MAINTENANCE. Immediate openings for clean-up people. Positions start at $9.00/hr. Applications accepted M–F 8 A.M. to 4:30 P.M. at Civic Center Administration Office, Danforth St. No phone calls please.

CLEANING PEOPLE. (14) Full-time. Will train. Call 293-9116

COUNTER PERSON (15) WANTED for pleasant new year-round sandwich and gift shop near East River Park. Call Jane or Lou at 748-1932

DIETARY AIDE (16)
Excellent working conditions and competitive wages.
Medical Center
475 Thomas St.
Rivertown

GAS STATION ATTENDANT. (17) Full-time. Uniforms provided.
Rivertown Service Station
293-8794

LAUNDRY HELPER (18)
Good at details. Willing to learn. Top wage for your right attitude.
PORT LAUNDRY
Hudson St., Rivertown
293-8012

LAWN SPRAYING—Hard worker needed. Better than average pay. Will train. (19) Beautiful Lawns, Inc., 17 Dakota St., Rivertown

LOCAL CLEANING (20) FIRM—Wants full-time people for night shift. Salary and benefits. Call 293-1761 or 293-8842, Monday–Friday 9–4.

Needed: Person to work in (21) Day Care Center. Must be good with children. High school education. References required. Call 748-1198

OFFICE DELIVERY— (22)
$8.00–$9.00/HR.
293-7126, Ext. 328

PAINTER—Need immedi- (23) ately for custom homes. Full time. Both inside and outside. Must have valid driver's license and own transportation. If interested, call 8–5.
Porter's Construction
293-0198

(24) RECEPTIONIST

This is an entry-level job for the person who can word process 45 wpm and has a pleasant telephone manner. We offer a competitive salary and an excellent benefit package. Apply to:

RIVERTOWN CITY HALL
1028 Spring Street

(continued)

Classified Ads: Help Wanted *(continued)*

(25) RETAIL SALES HELP Apply in person. Clothes to Go. The Mall, Danforth St., Rivertown 10–4. Ask for Mary.

(26) SEEKING highly motivated person to install carpets. Experience helpful but not necessary. 748-0028, leave message. Immediate openings.

(27) GAS STATION ATTENDANT—full time days. Mall area. Health ins. & paid vacation. 293-4861 10 A.M.–2 P.M. ONLY

(28) STOCKROOM/DELIVERY Person Wanted. Walchville printing company needs individual to work in stockroom and do deliveries. Must have driver's license and knowledge of area. Apply at:
Friendly Printer
84 Allen Street
Walchville

(29) TERMINAL WORKERS. Needed for loading and unloading. Second and third shifts. $9.10 to start. $10.00 after 60 days. Excellent benefits package. Full-time, steady work.
Call 293-2846
between 9 A.M.
and 3 P.M.

(30) WALCH RIVER HOTEL
River Drive and Fifth Street, Walchville
Room Attendant—General cleaning of hotel guest rooms. Excellent training program and excellent managers. Uniforms and employee meals. Schedule will include some weekends. Apply at the front desk.

(31)
HOUSEKEEPERS
$7.00 to $9.50/hr.

The Riverside Hotel is now hiring for permanent full-time positions. If you would like to work where the guest is our number one priority and the employee our number one asset, come by and apply. Apply in person Monday through Friday 10 A.M. to 3 P.M.

The Riverside Hotel
River Drive and Second St.
Walchville

(32)
MEADOW DAIRY NEEDS YOU

We have a truck-loading position for a motivated worker. Shift starts at 2 P.M. with pay starting at $9.50 per hour going to $10.00 after 60 days. We offer an excellent benefits package, which includes health, life, and dental insurance, profit sharing and paid vacations—just to name a few. If interested, apply at:

84 Clifton Street
Rivertown

(33–34)
RIVERTOWN GLASS
Utility Clerk/Driver

Driver's license, good driving record, and own vehicle required. Mileage paid. Duties include sorting and delivering mail, running errands, switchboard relief (will train), filing.

Window Assemblers

To work in busy factory. Will train you if you are ambitious, able to read a tape measure, and can read work orders.

Call 293-6339

(35)
Production Workers
2nd Shift
WE WILL TRAIN

Alitrode, a progressive electronics manufacturing firm is seeking candidates for existing and future production opportunities within our Wafer Fabrication departments for first shift (7 A.M. to 3:30 P.M.) and second shift (3:30 P.M. to midnight).

Check Us Out

- ☑ Paid Training
- ☑ Merit Pay Raises
- ☑ Advancement
- ☑ Full Benefits
- ☑ Modern Working Conditions

If interested, please stop by from 10 A.M. to 2 P.M. to fill out an application and have an interview.

Alitrode: 47 Sunset Circle, Rivertown

(36)
WANT MORE THAN A
DEAD-END JOB?

Come to Smith Paneling Inc., 18 Sunset Circle, Rivertown. We are a national leader in the manufacturing of paneling, and our plant is building its 2nd and 3rd shift. No special skills required except a willingness to learn. Be part of a great team!

Please apply at our office Mon.–Fri.

Explanations of Job Descriptions

The following nine pages are descriptions of the jobs listed in the classified ads. Below is an explanation of the information contained in each job description. See pages 15–19 for instructions on how to prepare and use these job descriptions.

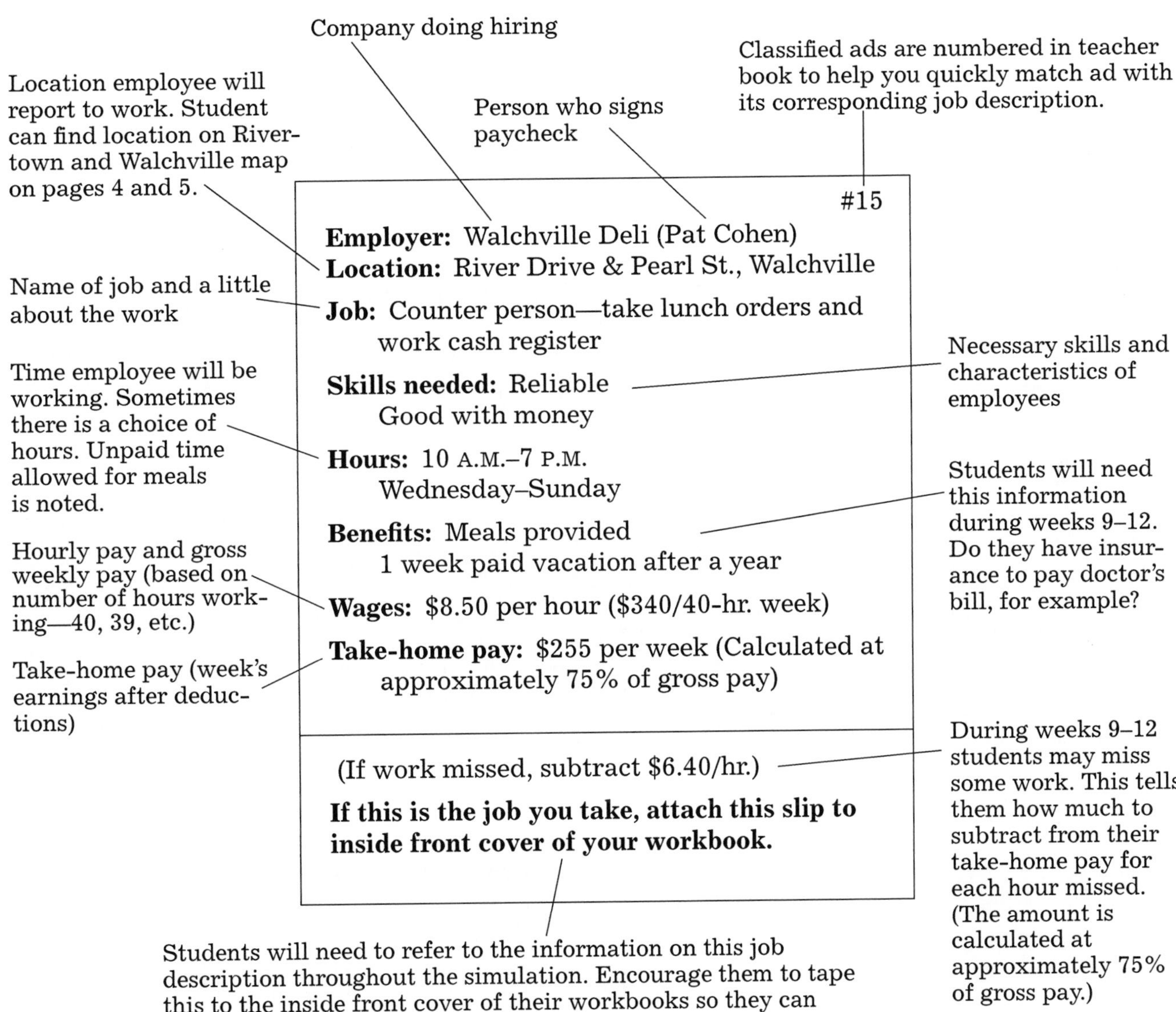

Company doing hiring
Classified ads are numbered in teacher book to help you quickly match ad with its corresponding job description.
Location employee will report to work. Student can find location on Rivertown and Walchville map on pages 4 and 5.
Person who signs paycheck
#15
Employer: Walchville Deli (Pat Cohen)
Location: River Drive & Pearl St., Walchville
Name of job and a little about the work
Job: Counter person—take lunch orders and work cash register
Necessary skills and characteristics of employees
Time employee will be working. Sometimes there is a choice of hours. Unpaid time allowed for meals is noted.
Skills needed: Reliable
Good with money
Hours: 10 A.M.–7 P.M.
Wednesday–Sunday
Students will need this information during weeks 9–12. Do they have insurance to pay doctor's bill, for example?
Benefits: Meals provided
1 week paid vacation after a year
Hourly pay and gross weekly pay (based on number of hours working—40, 39, etc.)
Wages: $8.50 per hour ($340/40-hr. week)
Take-home pay (week's earnings after deductions)
Take-home pay: $255 per week (Calculated at approximately 75% of gross pay)
During weeks 9–12 students may miss some work. This tells them how much to subtract from their take-home pay for each hour missed. (The amount is calculated at approximately 75% of gross pay.)
(If work missed, subtract $6.40/hr.)
If this is the job you take, attach this slip to inside front cover of your workbook.
Students will need to refer to the information on this job description throughout the simulation. Encourage them to tape this to the inside front cover of their workbooks so they can easily locate the information when it is needed.

Job Descriptions

Job #1

Employer: LoMein Restaurant (Sam Ling)

Location: Chad St., Rivertown

Job: Prep cook—prepare ingredients for chef to use in cooking dishes

Skills needed: Cooking experience helpful
Quick and with attention to details

Hours: 10 A.M.–1 P.M. and 3 P.M.–8 P.M.
Wednesday–Sunday

Benefits: 2 weeks paid vacation after 1 year

Wages: $9.00 per hour ($360/40-hr. week)

Take-home pay: $270 per week

(If work missed, subtract $6.75/hr.)

If you take this job, tape this description inside the front cover of your workbook.

Job #2

Employer: LoMein Restaurant (Sam Ling)

Location: Chad St., Rivertown

Job: Dishwasher

Skills needed: Responsible
Good worker

Hours: 2 P.M.–10 P.M.
Wednesday–Sunday

Benefits: 2 weeks paid vacation after 1 year

Wages: $7.00 per hour ($280/40-hr. week)

Take-home pay: $210 per week

(If work missed, subtract $5.25/hr.)

If you take this job, tape this description inside the front cover of your workbook.

Job #3

Employer: Speedy Auto Care (John Reed)

Location: 27 Sherman St., Rivertown

Job: Automotive technician—change oil filter and lubricate engine

Skills needed: Good with hands
Like working on cars

Hours: 7:30 A.M.–4:30 P.M.
Monday–Friday (1 unpaid hour for meal)

Benefits: Paid holidays
1 week paid vacation after 1 year

Wages: $8.00 per hour ($320/40-hr. week)

Take-home pay: $240 per week

(If work missed, subtract $6.00/hr.)

If you take this job, tape this description inside the front cover of your workbook.

Job #4

Employer: Rivertown Dodge (Bud Smith)

Location: Intersection of Congress & Jane Sts., Rivertown

Job: Auto reconditioning

Skills needed: Will train willing worker

Hours: 4:30 P.M.–1 A.M.
Monday–Friday (1/2 unpaid hour for meal)

Benefits: Health insurance
Paid holidays
2 weeks paid vacation after 1 year

Wages: $9.50/hour ($380/40-hr. week)

Take-home pay: $285 per week

(If work missed, subtract $7.13/hr.)

If you take this job, tape this description inside the front cover of your workbook.

Job Descriptions *(continued)*

#5

Job

Employer: Mill Co. (Sandra Johnson)

Location: 102 Kent St., Walchville

Job: Clerical assistant to help with office duties

Skills needed: Typing
Filing
Telephone skills
Word processing helpful

Hours: 8:30 A.M.–5 P.M.
Monday–Friday (½ unpaid hour for meal)

Benefits: Paid holidays
2 weeks paid vacation
Health insurance

Wages: $8.00 per hour ($320/40-hr. week)

Take-home pay: $240 per week

(If work missed, subtract $6.00/hr.)

If you take this job, tape this description inside the front cover of your workbook.

#6

Job

Employer: Walchville Health Care Facility (Dawn Sawyer)

Location: First Ave., Walchville

Job: Dietary aide—assist in meal preparation and serve meals to residents

Skills needed: Enjoy older people
Familiar with food preparation

Hours: 7 A.M.–10 A.M., Monday–Friday
and 7 A.M.–7:30 A.M., Saturday–Sunday
Alternate week: 7 A.M.–3 P.M., Monday–Friday

Benefits: 1 week paid vacation after 1 year

Wages: $8.00 per hour ($320/40-hr. week)

Take-home pay: $240 per week

(If work missed, subtract $6.00/hr.)

If you take this job, tape this description inside the front cover of your workbook.

#7

Job

Employer: Martin's Inn (Jo Lyons)

Location: 248 Clifton St., Rivertown

Job: Prep cook—prepare ingredients for cooking

Skills needed: Neat; good worker;
familiar with kitchen

Hours: 7:30 A.M.–1 P.M. Monday–Friday
and Saturday 8 A.M.–8:30 P.M.

Benefits: Health insurance
Time-and-a-half holidays
1 week paid vacation after 1 year

Wages: $9.00 per hour ($360/40-hr. week)

Take-home pay: $270 per week

(If work missed, subtract $6.75/hr.)

If you take this job, tape this description inside the front cover of your workbook.

#8

Job

Employer: Martin's Inn (Jo Lyons)

Location: 248 Clifton St., Rivertown

Job: Maid—clean guest rooms, make beds and refurbish supplies

Skills needed: Cleaning ability
Reliable

Hours: 7:30 A.M.–2 P.M.
Sunday–Friday

Benefits: Health insurance
Time-and-a-half for holidays
1 week paid vacation after 1 year

Wages: $7.50/hour ($300/40-hr. week)

Take-home pay: $225 per week

(If work missed, subtract $5.60/hr.)

If you take this job, tape this description inside the front cover of your workbook.

Job #9

Employer: Leavitt Awning Company (David Leavitt)

Location: Maple & Danforth Sts., Rivertown

Job: Awning technician—install awnings for home & business

Skills needed: Good with hands
Able to work from ladder

Hours: 7:30 A.M.–4 P.M.
Monday–Friday ($\frac{1}{2}$ unpaid hour for meal)

Benefits: Time-and-a-half overtime
Health insurance
2 weeks paid vacation after a year

Wages: $11.00 per hour ($440/40-hr. week)

Take-home pay: $330 per week

(If work missed, subtract $8.25/hr.)

If you take this job, tape this description inside the front cover of your workbook.

Job #10

Employer: Sweet Treats Bakery (Mary Russo)

Location: Rivertown Mall, Carter & Danforth Sts.

Job: Baker's assistant

Skills needed: Familiar with kitchen
Able to take directions
Lift heavy bags of flour

Hours: 4 A.M.–10:30 A.M., Monday–Saturday

Benefits: Health insurance
Paid holidays
1 week paid vacation after 1 year

Wages: $8.50 per hour ($331.50/39-hr. week)

Take-home pay: $250 per week

(If work missed, subtract $6.40/hr.)

If you take this job, tape this description inside the front cover of your workbook.

Job #11

Employer: Rivertown Redemption Center (George Baker)

Location: Corner of Maple and Longfellow Sts., Rivertown

Job: Bottle sorter

Skills needed: Quick worker

Hours: 8 A.M.–2 P.M., Monday–Friday
and 8 A.M.–6 P.M., Saturday

Benefits: Time-and-a-half overtime
1 week paid vacation after a year

Wages: $7.50 per hour ($300/40-hr. week)

Take-home pay: $225 per week

(If work missed, subtract $5.60/hr.)

If you take this job, tape this description inside the front cover of your workbook.

Job #12

Employer: Bill's Carpentry (Bill Singer)

Location: Fifth St. at Boyd St., Walchville

Job: Carpenter's helper

Skills needed: Familiarity with tools helpful
Good at taking directions
Must have own car

Hours: 8 A.M.–4:30 P.M.
Monday–Friday ($\frac{1}{2}$ unpaid hour for meal)

Benefits: 2 weeks paid vacation after a year
Paid holidays

Wages: $8.50 per hour ($340/40-hr. week)

Take-home pay: $255 per week

(If work missed, subtract $6.40/hr.)

If you take this job, tape this description inside the front cover of your workbook.

Job #13

Employer: Civic Center (Sandy Edwards)

Location: Danforth St., between Coyle & Eliot Sts., Rivertown

Job: Custodian—set up and clean up after events; heavy lifting

Skills needed: Good health and strength
Reliable

Hours: 8 A.M.–4:30 P.M.
Wednesday–Sunday (1/2 unpaid hour for meal)

Benefits: Health insurance
1 week paid vacation after 6 months

Wages: $9.00/hour ($360/40-hr. week)

Take-home pay: $270 per week

(If work missed, subtract $6.75/hr.)

If you take this job, tape this description inside the front cover of your workbook.

Job #14

Employer: Allied Business Cleaners (Rose Myers)

Location: Intersection of Franklin & Walnut Sts., Rivertown

Job: Office cleaner

Skills needed: Careful worker

Hours: 8 P.M.–6 A.M.
Monday–Thursday

Benefits: 1 week paid vacation after 1 year

Wages: $8.00 per hour ($320/40-hr. week)

Take-home pay: $240 per week

(If work missed, subtract $6.00/hr.)

If you take this job, tape this description inside the front cover of your workbook.

Job #15

Employer: Walchville Deli (Pat Cohen)

Location: River Drive & Pearl St., Walchville

Job: Counter person—take lunch orders and work cash register

Skills needed: Reliable
Good with money

Hours: 10 A.M.–7 P.M.
Wednesday–Sunday (1 unpaid hour for meal)

Benefits: Meals provided
1 week paid vacation after a year

Wages: $8.50 per hour ($340/40-hr. week)

Take-home pay: $255 per week

(If work missed, subtract $6.40/hr.)

If you take this job, tape this description inside the front cover of your workbook.

Job #16

Employer: Medical Center (Steve Otis)

Location: 475 Thomas St., Rivertown

Job: Dietary aide—serve meals to patients

Skills needed: Friendly with people
Neat and reliable

Hours: 6 A.M.–2 P.M.
Tuesday–Saturday

Benefits: Health insurance
Holiday pay
2 weeks paid vacation after a year

Wages: $8.00 per hour ($320/40-hr. week)

Take-home pay: $240 per week

(If work missed, subtract $6.00/hr.)

If you take this job, tape this description inside the front cover of your workbook.

Job #17

Employer: Rivertown Service Station (Shawn Ducharme)

Location: Franklin St. & Holly Ave., Rivertown

Job: Gas station attendant—pump gas, check under the hood, wash windshields, etc.

Skills needed: Friendly
Money skills

Hours: 8 A.M.–5 P.M.
Tuesday–Saturday (1 unpaid hour for meal)

Benefits: Uniforms provided
Health insurance
2 weeks paid vacation after a year

Wages: $7.50/hour ($300/40-hr. week)

Take-home pay: $225 per week

(If work missed, subtract $5.65/hr.)

If you take this job, tape this description inside the front cover of your workbook.

Job #18

Employer: Port Laundry (Alicia Cook)

Location: Hudson St., Rivertown

Job: Laundry helper

Skills needed: Take directions
Basic math

Hours: 7:30 A.M.–4 P.M.
Monday–Friday (½ unpaid hour for meal)

Benefits: Health insurance
1 week paid vacation after 1 year

Wages: $8.00 per hour ($320/40-hr. week)

Take-home pay: $240 per week

(If work missed, subtract $6.00/hr.)

If you take this job, tape this description inside the front cover of your workbook.

Job #19

Employer: Beautiful Lawns, Inc. (Jean Corcoran)

Location: 17 Dakota St., Rivertown

Job: Lawn spraying

Skills needed: Like to work outside
Good health

Hours: 7:30 A.M.–4 P.M.
Monday–Friday (½ unpaid hour for meal)

Benefits: Health insurance

Wages: $10.00 per hour ($400/40-hr. week)

Take-home pay: $300 per week

(If work missed, subtract $7.50/hr.)

If you take this job, tape this description inside the front cover of your workbook.

Job #20

Employer: Mac's Cleaning Service (Sue MacDonald)

Location: Cumberland & Forest Aves., Rivertown

Job: Cleaning offices and professional buildings after hours

Skills needed: Good worker
Get along with others

Hours: 4 P.M.–midnight
Monday–Friday

Benefits: Health insurance
2 weeks paid vacation after a year

Wages: $8.00 per hour ($320/40-hr. week)

Take-home pay: $240 per week

(If work missed, subtract $6.00/hr.)

If you take this job, tape this description inside the front cover of your workbook.

Job Descriptions *(continued)*

Job #21

Employer: Walchville Day Care Center (Gerry Willis)

Location: Fourth St. & 3rd Ave., Walchville

Job: Assistant to teacher—work with children; prepare breakfast and lunch

Skills needed: Patience with children
Cooking skills
Able to work with others
High school education

Hours: 7 A.M.–4 P.M.
Monday–Friday (1 unpaid hour for meal)

Benefits: Health insurance
Paid holidays

Wages: $7.00/hour ($280/40-hr. week)

Take-home pay: $210 per week

(If work missed, subtract $5.25/hr.)

If you take this job, tape this description inside the front cover of your workbook.

Job #22

Employer: Downtown Courier (Skip Ellis)

Location: High & Congress Sts., Rivertown

Job: Office delivery by bicycle

Skills needed: Reliable
Able to ride bicycle

Hours: 9 A.M.–5 P.M.
Monday–Friday

Benefits: Health insurance
Paid holidays

Wages: $8.00/hour ($320/40-hr. week)
OR $9.00/hour ($360/40-hr. week)

Take-home pay: $240/week OR $270/week

Note: Lower wage 8 weeks; then pay increase to higher wage

(If work missed, subtract $6.00/hr. or $6.75/hr.)

If you take this job, tape this description inside the front cover of your workbook.

Job #23

Employer: Porter's Construction Company (Dan Porter)

Location: Eliot & Congress Sts., Rivertown

Job: Painter—interior & exterior

Skills needed: Careful worker—neat and reliable
Painting experience helpful
Valid driver's license
Own transportation

Hours: 8 A.M.–5 P.M.
Monday–Friday (1 unpaid hour for meal)

Benefits: 2 weeks paid vacation after 1 year

Wages: $11.00 per hour ($440/40-hr. week)

Take-home pay: $330 per week

(If work missed, subtract $8.25/hr.)

If you take this job, tape this description inside the front cover of your workbook.

Job #24

Employer: Rivertown City Hall (Dorothy Clark)

Location: 1028 Spring St. (between Park & High Sts.), Rivertown

Job: Receptionist

Skills needed: Word processing (45 wpm)
Pleasant telephone manner

Hours: 8:30 A.M.–5 P.M.
Monday–Friday (½ unpaid hour for meal)

Benefits: Health and dental insurance
Paid holidays
Two weeks paid vacation after a year

Wages: $8.50 per hour ($340/40-hr. week)

Take-home pay: $255 per week

(If work missed, subtract $6.40/hr.)

If you take this job, tape this description inside the front cover of your workbook.

Job #25

Employer: Clothes to Go (Sally Love)

Location: Rivertown Mall (Holly Ave. & Danforth St., Rivertown)

Job: Retail sales—help customers and handle sales

Skills needed: Neat
Pleasant with customers
Basic math

Hours: 9:30 A.M.–6 P.M.
Tuesday–Saturday (½ unpaid hour for meal)

Benefits: Paid holidays
1 week paid vacation after 1 year

Wages: $7.50/hour ($300/40-hr. week)

Take-home pay: $225 per week

(If work missed, subtract $5.63/hr.)

If you take this job, tape this description inside the front cover of your workbook.

Job #26

Employer: Interior Designs (John Stover)

Location: David & Robinson Sts., Walchville

Job: Carpet installer

Skills needed: Hardworking
Carpet experience helpful, but not necessary

Hours: 8 A.M.–4:30 P.M.
Monday–Friday (½ unpaid hour for meal)

Benefits: Paid holidays

Wages: $10.50 per hour ($420/40-hr. week)

Take-home pay: $315 per week

(If work missed, subtract $7.88/hr.)

If you take this job, tape this description inside the front cover of your workbook.

Job #27

Employer: Steve's Service Station (Steve Carter)

Location: Congress St. at Holly Ave., Rivertown

Job: Service station attendant

Skills needed: Friendly
Like working on cars
Make change

Hours: Noon–8:30 P.M.
Monday–Friday (½ unpaid hour for meal)

Benefits: 2 weeks paid vacation after 1 year
Health insurance

Wages: $9.00 per hour ($360/40-hr. week)

Take-home pay: $270 per week

(If work missed, subtract $6.75/hr.)

If you take this job, tape this description inside the front cover of your workbook.

Job #28

Employer: Friendly Printer (Russell Taylor)

Location: 84 Allen St., Walchville

Job: Stockroom & delivery person

Skills needed: Driver's license
Knowledge of area
Ability to lift and carry heavy loads

Hours: 8:30 A.M.–5 P.M.
Monday–Friday (½ unpaid hour for meal)

Benefits: Health insurance
2 weeks paid vacation after 1 year

Wages: $9.50 per hour ($380/40-hr. week)

Take-home pay: $285 per week

(If work missed, subtract $7.15/hr.)

If you take this job, tape this description inside the front cover of your workbook.

Job #29

Employer: Marshall Wharf (Tony Sawyer)

Location: Walch River at end of Hudson St., Rivertown

Job: Terminal workers—loading and unloading

Skills needed: Good health
Strong

Hours: 4 P.M.–midnight, Monday–Friday
OR midnight–8 A.M., Monday–Friday

Benefits: Health & dental insurance
2 weeks paid vacation
Paid holidays

Wages: \$9.10 per hour (\$364/40-hr. week)
OR \$10.00 per hour (\$400/40-hr. week)

Take-home pay: \$273 per week
OR \$300 per week

Note: Lower wage 8 weeks; then pay increase to higher wage

(If work missed, subtract \$6.83/hr. OR \$7.50/hr.)

If you take this job, tape this description inside the front cover of your workbook.

Job #30

Employer: Walch River Hotel (Dick Harvey)

Location: River Drive & 5th St., Walchville

Job: Room attendant—cleaning hotel guest rooms

Skills needed: Fast worker
Get along with others

Hours: 8 A.M.–4:30 P.M.
Tuesday–Saturday (1/2 unpaid hour for meal)

Benefits: Uniforms
Meals while on duty
Health insurance
2 weeks paid vacation after a year

Wages: \$7.50 per hour (\$300/40-hr. week)

Take-home pay: \$225 per week

(If work missed, subtract \$5.65/hr.)

If you take this job, tape this description inside the front cover of your workbook.

Job #31

Employer: Riverside Hotel (Angela Lyons)

Location: River Drive and Second St., Walchville

Job: Housekeeper

Skills needed: Good cleaning ability
Fast worker

Hours: 8 A.M.–4:30 P.M.
Wednesday–Sunday (1/2 unpaid hour for meal)

Benefits: Time-and-a-half holidays
Health insurance
1 week paid vacation after 6 months

Wages: \$8.00 per hour (\$320/40-hr. week)

Take-home pay: \$240 per week

(If work missed, subtract \$6.00/hr.)

If you take this job, tape this description inside the front cover of your workbook.

Job #32

Employer: Meadow Dairy (Lin Marshall)

Location: 84 Clifton St., Rivertown

Job: Loading trucks

Skills needed: Ability to lift heavy cartons
Dependable

Hours: 2 P.M.–10 P.M.
Monday–Friday

Benefits: Health, life, and dental insurance
2 weeks paid vacation
Paid holidays
Profit sharing after 2 years

Wages: \$9.50 per hour (\$380/40-hr. week)
OR \$10.00 per hour (\$400/40-hr. week) after 60 days

Take-home pay: \$285 per week OR \$300 per week

(If work missed, subtract \$7.15/hr. OR \$7.50/hr.)

If you take this job, tape this description inside the front cover of your workbook.

Job #33

Employer: Rivertown Glass (Chris Davis)

Location: Park & Commercial Sts., Rivertown

Job: Utility clerk/driver

Skills needed: Driver's license—must have own vehicle
Dependable
Switchboard (will train)
Filing

Hours: 8:30 A.M.–5 P.M.
Monday–Friday (½ unpaid hour for meal)

Benefits: Health insurance
Paid holidays
2 weeks paid vacation after 1 year

Wages: \$8.50 per hour (\$340/40-hr. week)

Take-home pay: \$255 per week

(If work missed, subtract \$6.40/hr.)

If you take this job, tape this description inside the front cover of your workbook.

Job #34

Employer: Rivertown Glass (John Yorke)

Location: Park & Commercial Sts., Rivertown

Job: Window assembler

Skills needed: Willing to learn
Measure accurately
Read work orders

Hours: 7:30 A.M.–4 P.M.
Monday–Friday (½ unpaid hour for meal)

Benefits: Health insurance
Paid holidays
Two weeks paid vacation after 1 year

Wages: \$12.00 per hour (\$480/40-hr. week)

Take-home pay: \$360 per week

(If work missed, subtract \$9.00/hr.)

If you take this job, tape this description inside the front cover of your workbook.

Job #35

Employer: Alitrode (Alan Herrick)

Location: 47 Sunset Circle, Rivertown

Job: Production worker for wafer fabrication

Skills needed: Careful worker
Good with hands

Hours: 7 A.M.–3:30 P.M., Monday–Friday
(½ unpaid hour for meal)
OR 3:30 P.M.–midnight, Monday–Friday
(½ unpaid hour for meal)

Benefits: Health and dental insurance
Paid holidays
1 week paid vacation after a year

Wages: \$9.50 per hour (\$380/40-hr. week)

Take-home pay: \$285 per week

(If work missed, subtract \$7.15/hr.)

If you take this job, tape this description inside the front cover of your workbook.

Job #36

Employer: Smith Paneling Inc. (Tom Richards)

Location: 18 Sunset Circle, Rivertown

Job: Panel manufacturing

Skills needed: Willingness to learn

Hours: 5 P.M.–1 A.M., Monday–Friday
OR 1 A.M.–9 A.M., Monday–Friday

Benefits: Health insurance
1 week paid vacation
Paid holidays

Wages: \$9.00/hr. 2nd shift (\$360/40-hr. week)
\$10.00/hr. 3rd shift (\$400/40-hr. week)

Take-home pay: \$270/wk. 2nd shift
\$300/wk. 3rd shift

(If work missed, subtract \$6.75/hr. 2nd shift or \$7.50/hr. 3rd shift)

If you take this job, tape this description inside the front cover of your workbook.

4. Application for Employment

COMPANY OR EMPLOYER ____________ JOB TITLE ____________

APPLICATION FOR EMPLOYMENT

(AN EQUAL OPPORTUNITY EMPLOYER)

1. PERSONAL INFORMATION

DATE

SOCIAL SECURITY NUMBER

NAME (LAST / FIRST / MIDDLE)

PRESENT ADDRESS (STREET / CITY / STATE / ZIP)

PERMANENT ADDRESS (STREET / CITY / STATE / ZIP)

DAYTIME PHONE NO. HOME PHONE IF DIFFERENT ARE YOU 18 YEARS OR OLDER? Yes ☐ No ☐

2. DRIVING

DO YOU HAVE A DRIVER'S LICENSE? YES ☐ NO ☐

DO YOU HAVE A COMMERCIAL DRIVER'S LICENSE? YES ☐ NO ☐

STATE WHERE YOU GOT YOUR LICENSE ____________

3. EMPLOYMENT DESIRED

POSITION DATE YOU CAN START SALARY DESIRED

ARE YOU EMPLOYED NOW? IF SO, MAY WE INQUIRE OF YOUR PRESENT EMPLOYER? EVER APPLIED TO THIS COMPANY BEFORE? WHEN?

AVAILABILITY FOR WORK: ☐ FULL-TIME ☐ PART-TIME ☐ TEMPORARY

HOURS AVAILABLE: ________ TO ________ DAYS ____________

HOW DID YOU HEAR ABOUT THIS POSITION? ____________

4. EDUCATION	NAME AND LOCATION OF SCHOOL	NO. OF YEARS ATTENDED	DID YOU GRADUATE?	SUBJECTS STUDIED
HIGH SCHOOL				
COLLEGE				
TRADE OR BUSINESS SCHOOL				

5. GENERAL

U.S. MILITARY SERVICE RANK PRESENT MEMBERSHIP IN NATIONAL GUARD OR RESERVES

PLEASE INDICATE ANY SPECIAL SKILLS AND/OR QUALIFICATIONS YOU POSSESS THAT YOU FEEL RELATE DIRECTLY TO THE POSITION FOR WHICH YOU ARE APPLYING (TYPING, SPECIAL LICENSES OR CERTIFICATIONS, COMPUTER KNOWLEDGE, MACHINE SKILLS, ETC.).

____

____

(continued)

4. Application for Employment *(continued)*

6. FORMER EMPLOYERS LIST BELOW YOUR LAST FOUR EMPLOYERS, STARTING WITH THE LAST ONE FIRST.

DATE MONTH & YEAR	NAME AND ADDRESS OF EMPLOYER	SALARY/ POSITION	RESPONSIBILITIES	REASON FOR LEAVING
FROM				
TO				
FROM				
TO				
FROM				
TO				
FROM				
TO				

7. REFERENCES GIVE THE NAMES OF THREE PERSONS NOT RELATED TO YOU, WHOM YOU HAVE KNOWN AT LEAST ONE YEAR.

NAME	ADDRESS	BUSINESS	YEARS ACQUAINTED
1			
2			
3			

8. OTHER COMMENTS

9. PROSPECTIVE EMPLOYEES WILL RECEIVE CONSIDERATION WITHOUT DISCRIMINATION BECAUSE OF RACE, CREED, COLOR, SEX, AGE, NATIONAL ORIGIN, OR HANDICAP. COMPLETION OF THIS APPLICATION DOES NOT IMPLY OR WARRANT THAT THE APPLICANT WILL BE CONSIDERED FOR A POSITION IN THE COMPANY.

"I CERTIFY THAT THE FACTS CONTAINED IN THIS APPLICATION ARE TRUE AND COMPLETE TO THE BEST OF MY KNOWLEDGE AND UNDERSTAND THAT, IF EMPLOYED, FALSIFIED STATEMENTS ON THIS APPLICATION SHALL BE GROUNDS FOR DISMISSAL.

"I AUTHORIZE INVESTIGATION OF ALL STATEMENTS CONTAINED HEREIN AND THE REFERENCES LISTED ABOVE TO GIVE YOU ANY AND ALL INFORMATION CONCERNING MY PREVIOUS EMPLOYMENT AND ANY PERTINENT INFORMATION THEY MAY HAVE, PERSONAL OR OTHERWISE, AND RELEASE ALL PARTIES FROM ALL LIABILITY FOR ANY DAMAGE THAT MAY RESULT FROM FURNISHING SAME TO YOU.

"I UNDERSTAND AND AGREE THAT, IF HIRED, MY EMPLOYMENT IS FOR NO DEFINITE PERIOD AND MAY, REGARDLESS OF THE DATE OF PAYMENT OF MY WAGES AND SALARY, BE TERMINATED AT ANY TIME WITHOUT ANY PRIOR NOTICE."

DATE SIGNATURE

Student page 10

Answers will vary

2. The Right Job for You

What kind of job do you want? This page can help you find out. Answer these questions:

1. Where do you want to work?
   - ❑ Outdoors ❑ Inside
2. Do you want to work with people?
   - ❑ Yes. ❑ No. I work best alone.
3. Do you get bored often?
   - ❑ I can do the same thing all day. ❑ I need variety in my work.
4. What about schedule?
   - ❑ I want weekends off. ❑ I'll work anytime.
5. How is your health?
   - ❑ I can do any job. ❑ There are some things I can't do.
6. Can you stay awake at night?
   - ❑ No. I want to work days. ❑ Yes. I could work nights.
7. Is money important to you?
   - ❑ Yes. I want high pay. ❑ No. High pay doesn't matter.
8. What can you do?

❑ Type	❑ Cook	❑ Learn fast
❑ Drive	❑ Fix cars	❑ Work fast
❑ Read	❑ Carpentry	❑ Math
❑ File	❑ Paint	❑ Use a computer
❑ Clean	❑ Run a cash register	❑ ____________
❑ Work well with people	❑ Laundry	❑ ____________
❑ Answer a phone	❑ Lift things	❑ ____________

9. What special interests do you have that might help on a job?
   I like ________________________________
10. What are some jobs you might like? ________________________________

Student page 13

Answers will vary

3. Job Hunting in the Classifieds

Use the help-wanted ads on pages 11 and 12 to complete the items below.

1. Find three jobs that would require being outdoors. ____________
2. List two jobs that require working with the public. ____________
3. Find a job you might enjoy if you like to work with children. ____________
4. What are two jobs you would need math skills to do? ____________
5. Many ads tell only a little about the job. How can you learn more? ____________
6. List one job that asks you to apply in person. ____________
7. Find a job that asks you to call for more information. ____________
8. All employers offer pay. Some also offer benefits like health insurance and vacation. Choose two ads and list the benefits they talk about.
   ____
9. Find two ads that are a lot alike. Read the ads; then fill in this chart.

	Job #1	Job #2
Hours:		
Pay:		
Benefits:		

10. Choose three jobs that you might like to apply for.
    - Job 1 ____________
    - Job 2 ____________
    - Job 3 ____________

Student pages 14–15

Answers will vary

See teacher book pages 33–34

Student page 16

Sample

5. Week 1—Living on Your Own

for Lee West

What is your job? Gas Station Attendant

Who is your employer? Rivertown Service Station (Shawn Ducharme)

What is the address where you work? Franklin St. & Center Ave., Rivertown

What days do you work? Tuesday-Saturday

What are your hours each day? 8 a.m.-5 p.m.

How many hours do you work each week? 40

What is your hourly rate of pay? $7.50

What is your weekly gross pay? $300

What is your take-home pay each week? $225

What benefits do you receive? uniforms, health insurance, 2 weeks paid vacation after a year

Fill out a time card for your first week of work.

Write your name on the top line.

How many hours did you work on Monday? Write only the hours worked. Do not include time for meals.

List the number of hours worked each day.

Add the total number of hours worked this week.

Time Card

Employee: Lee West

Day	Hours
Monday	
Tuesday	8
Wednesday	8
Thursday	8
Friday	8
Saturday	8
Sunday	
TOTAL:	40

Part 3: Taking Care of Your Money

Part 3: Taking Care of Your Money

Objectives

- Students will imagine visiting a bank to talk about accounts.
- Students will practice writing checks and keeping a check register.
- Students will explore the benefits of a savings account.
- Students will begin planning a budget they can use for this simulation.
- Students will complete the second week of the simulation.

Materials Needed

Activity 6: Going to a Bank
Activity 7: A Savings Account
Activity 8: A Checking Account
Activity 9: Plan Your Budget
Activity 10: Week 2—Living on Your Own

Pre-teaching

Be sure students understand these words related to the general topic of handling money: *bank, savings, checking, account,* and *budget.*

Review vocabulary associated with individual activities either before using them or while going through them with the class. Challenging terms include: Activity 6—*overdraft protection, credit card,* and *application;* Activity 7—*interest, original, unexpected,* and *emergency;* Activity 8—*check register, deposit, balance, numerals, subtract, electricity, description, transaction, payment,* and *debt;* Activity 9—*estimate, category, adjusted figures, utilities, transportation, insurance, medical, predict,* and *medication;* Activity 10—*payable.*

Commentary: Introduction

You have started work and the money will soon be coming in. What will you do with that first paycheck?

You could just cash the check and put all the money in your pocket. Why isn't this a good plan?

It's easy to lose the money.
You can spend it on things you don't want or need.
You have no record of where the money went.
You might not have money to pay bills.

Commentary: Activity 6: Going to a Bank

People who have jobs and earn money often use banks. They put their money into savings accounts or checking accounts. What is one good way to find out about banks and their services?

Going to the bank and asking

A lot of people feel nervous the first time they go to a bank. But you don't need to. The people in the bank are paid to help you. They know your money is important to you, and they want to help you make good decisions about how to handle it. Look at Activity 6. Read what it says, and make your decisions. Then we'll talk about your answers.

Commentary: Activity 7: A Savings Account

If you put your money in the bank, you might choose to put it in a savings account. Why might it be a good idea to put some money in a savings account?

Savings accounts pay interest.

Look at Activity 7: A Savings Account. Answer the questions to find out a little more about a savings account.

Commentary: Activity 8: A Checking Account

What can you tell me about a checking account?

You put money in the bank and write checks to spend it.
If you spend more than you have, checks "bounce."
You have to keep records of checks written and deposits made.
The bank sends statements to you so you have a record of payments.

Look at pages 20 and 21. There are three checks and a check register. You are going to use these as you do the activity on the previous page. It tells about Lee West using a checking account.

Commentary: Activity 9: Plan Your Budget

We've talked about checking accounts and savings accounts, but the thing we need to talk about now is a plan for managing your money. And that plan is called a budget.

Look at Activity 9: Plan Your Budget. You will see that there are two major parts to a budget. What are they?

Income
Expenses

For this simulation, you know pretty much what your income will be. What is your weekly take-home pay? Write the amount on the line.

Now the trick of a budget is to make sure your expenses are not greater than this income.

Budgets can be done on a weekly, monthly, or yearly basis. Think about this budget in terms of weekly expenses.

What will be the major expenses in your budget?

Housing
Food
Transportation
Clothes
Insurance and medical
Savings
Fun and entertainment
Other

Estimate (take an educated guess) how much you will spend weekly on each of these items. Fill in the column under "Estimated Budget." Be sure your estimated budget total is not more than your actual income. We'll be filling in the adjusted budget in the weeks to come as we learn more about the expenses of living on your own.

It is important to remember that a budget is always flexible and changing. You may get a raise that would increase your income. Or your rent may be increased so that your expenses are higher. One week you may have a doctor's appointment and a really low grocery bill. Another week you may entertain friends and have a high grocery bill.

A budget is a helpful guide. But to be most helpful, it is flexible.

Commentary: Activity 10: Week 2—Living on Your Own

In the first week of the simulation, you made out your time card. So what do you expect will happen this second week?

Get paid!

Look at Activity 10: Week 2—Living on Your Own. At the top of the page is your paycheck. Of course you aren't usually the one who writes your paycheck, but you will today. Follow the directions to:

- Make out your paycheck.
- Make a deposit in your checking account.
- Make a deposit in your savings account.
- Fill out your time card for your second week on the job.

Evaluation

Check student progress and understanding by reviewing completed workbook pages. Ask questions like these, using some to help students understand how they can apply their developing skills to their own lives.

- Are bank accounts a good idea for most people?
- Who in the class uses a budget? Do you stick to it? Does it help?
- What are good budgets like? (*Accurate, realistic, flexible.*)
- How can you avoid bouncing a check? (*Keep good records.*)
- Why do you think people have a lot of trouble saving money?

Extension Activities

Ask students to visit local banks and collect information about accounts for the class to share. Arrange a class field trip to visit a bank and talk with a representative about opening accounts. Ask students to report on their experience using local banks. Talk about the best way to choose a bank. Discuss the difference between debit cards and credit cards. (*Debit cards are something like checks. When you use them, the money is subtracted from your bank account. When you use a credit card, you owe the money until you pay with a check or in some other way.*) Get some sample application forms from local banks, and have students practice filling them out. Expand the class discussion of budgets by speaking of topics like *wants versus needs, short-term versus long-term goals,* and *fixed versus flexible expenses.* Introduce students to the idea of banking over the Internet. If you know something about this topic and have the facilities, demonstrate how they can find banks and banking information using computers.

Student page 18

Answers will vary

6. Going to a Bank

What do you want from a bank? Imagine that you go for a visit. A banker tells you what the bank can do for you, then asks what you want. Read what the banker says and answer the questions:

Banker: Do you want a savings account? That's a good way to make your money grow. But you need to leave your money in the bank for a while to make that happen.

What do you say? ☐ Yes, I want a savings account. ☐ No, I don't.

What is one reason for your answer? ____________

Banker: How about a checking account? That's a good way to keep your money safe. But you can also use it anytime you want.

What do you say? ☐ Yes, I want a checking account. ☐ No, I don't.

What is one reason for your answer? ____________

Banker: We also offer overdraft protection. An overdraft happens when you write a check for more money than you have in the bank. If you do that and you have protection, we will help you. If you don't have protection, you will have to pay out extra money.

What do you say? ☐ Yes, I want protection. ☐ No, I don't.

What is one reason for your answer? ____________

Banker: Do you need a debit card? You can buy things with a debit card if you want. The money for your purchases is automatically taken out of your account. You can also use the card to get cash or check your account balance at teller machines.

What do you say? ☐ Yes, I want a debit card. ☐ No, I don't.

What is one reason for your answer? ____________

Banker: Do you want to bank with us? Can I give you an application form to fill out?

What do you say? ☐ Yes, I want to bank with you. ☐ No, I don't.

What is one thing to think about when you choose a bank? ____________

Student page 19

7. A Savings Account

1. About a savings account:
   (a) If you put $100 in a hiding place and leave it there, how much will you have in a year? $100 if it stays there; nothing if it is lost or stolen
   (b) If you put $100 in a savings account at 6% interest, how much will you have in a year? (6% of $100 = .06 × $100 = $6.00.) Add the interest to the original amount. $106
   (c) Would you rather have $100 or $106? $106
2. Reasons to save:
   (a) Put an X beside the reasons why some people might keep their money in a savings account. *These could all be good reasons to save.*

   ___ To keep money safe
   ___ In case they lose their job
   ___ For a special purchase
   ___ So it won't get stolen
   ___ For a vacation
   ___ For an unexpected illness
   ___ So they won't spend it
   ___ For an emergency
   ___ It's a good habit
   ___ For new clothes
   ___ To make their money "grow"
   ___ To buy gifts

   (b) List three reasons why you might want to save your money. *Answers will vary*

   ____________ ____________ ____________
3. How to save:
   (a) Amanda saved $10 every week for a year. At the end of a year (52 weeks), how much money did she have in her savings account?
   $520, plus interest
   (b) Stan makes less money and has more expenses than Amanda. So he is only able to save $2.50 each week. How much will Stan have in his savings account at the end of a year?
   $130, plus interest
   (c) How much money would you like to try to save each week? *Answers will vary*
   (d) If you are able to save that amount each week, how much will you have in your savings account at the end of a year?
   Answers will vary, plus interest

Student page 20

8. A Checking Account

Make out the checks and keep a check register for Lee West. Checks are on the next page.

1. On October 3rd, Lee made a deposit of $300.
   Fill out the check register:
   (a) Write the date in the check register.
   (b) Write the amount of the deposit.
   (c) Under "balance," write the total amount in the account.
2. On October 5th, Lee wrote the first check, paying $250 to Gloria Brown for a deposit on an apartment.
   Write the check:
   (a) Write check number "1."
   (b) Write the date on the check.
   (c) Make the check out to Gloria Brown.
   (d) Write the amount of the check in numerals and words.
   (e) Sign the check.
   (f) Make a note about what the check is for beside "Memo."
   Fill out the check register:
   (a) Write the number of the check used.
   (b) Write the date.
   (c) Tell to whom the check was written and why.
   (d) Write the amount of the payment.
   (e) To get the new balance, subtract the amount of the payment from the old balance.
3. On October 10th, Lee made a deposit of $300.
   Fill out the check register:
   (a) Write the date in the check register.
   (b) Write the amount of the deposit.
   (c) To find the new balance, add the amount of the deposit to the old balance.
4. On October 12th, Lee paid $75 to the Power and Light Co. to get the electricity turned on.
   (a) Write the check.
   (b) Fill out the check register.
5. On October 14th, Lee shopped for groceries at Bud's Market and paid by check. The groceries cost $62.27.
   (a) Write the check.
   (b) Fill out the check register.

RECORD ALL CHARGES OR CREDITS THAT AFFECT YOUR ACCOUNT

NUMBER	DATE	DESCRIPTION OF TRANSACTION	PAYMENT/DEBIT (−)	√ T	FEE (IF ANY)	DEPOSIT/CREDIT (+)	BALANCE $
	Oct 3	Deposit				$300 —	$300 —
1	Oct 5	Gloria Brown (apt. deposit)	$250 —				$ 50 —
	Oct 10	Deposit				$300 —	$350 —
2	Oct 12	Power & Light Company (electricity)	$ 75 —				$275 —
3	Oct 14	Bud's Market (Groceries)	$ 62 27				$212 73

(continued)

Student page 21

8. A Checking Account *(continued)*

CHECK NO. 1
Oct 5 20 01 71-587/749
PAY TO THE ORDER OF Gloria Brown $ 250 —
Two hundred fifty and 00/100 DOLLARS
FIRST NATIONAL BANK
MEMO apartment deposit *Lee West*
⑆074905872⑆ 251⑈372⑈8⑈ 4311

CHECK NO. 2
Oct 12 20 01 71-587/749
PAY TO THE ORDER OF Power & Light Co. $ 75 —
Seventy-five and 00/100 DOLLARS
FIRST NATIONAL BANK
MEMO electricity turned on *Lee West*
⑆074905872⑆ 251⑈372⑈8⑈ 4311

CHECK NO. 3
Oct 14 20 01 71-587/749
PAY TO THE ORDER OF Bud's Market $ 62.27
Sixty-two and 27/100 DOLLARS
FIRST NATIONAL BANK
MEMO groceries *Lee West*
⑆074905872⑆ 251⑈372⑈8⑈ 4311

Student page 22

Sample **9. Plan Your Budget**

Your budget is your financial plan. It has two parts. The first is called "income." It shows the money you earn. The second is called "expenses." It shows how you think you will spend your money.

Income

What is your weekly take-home pay? $225.–

Expenses

Some major expenses are listed and explained below. Think about your income. Then decide how much you will spend in each category every week. Write your answers under "Estimated Budget." Don't write anything under "Adjusted Budget." You will put some answers there on another day.

Item	Estimated Budget	Adjusted Budget
Housing (rent & utilities) is one of the biggest expenses. Try to keep this between $\frac{1}{4}$ and $\frac{1}{3}$ of your income.	$ 75	
Food can be another large expense. How much you spend depends on how often you eat out and what you eat at home.	$ 55	
Transportation includes bus fare or car payments, gas, repairs, and insurance if you own a car.	$ 25	
Clothes expenses will depend on how you like to dress, how you have to dress for work, and if you get free uniforms at work.	$ 30	
Insurance/Medical expenses are sometimes hard to guess. Some employers pay health insurance. If you pay for your own, it can be expensive. It is difficult to predict when you will be sick or need medication.	$ 10	
Savings are for something special or for a "rainy day." The best way to save is to decide on a certain amount that you will save each week. (See Activity 7.)	$ 6	
Fun/Entertainment is also important. Decide how much you will budget for things like movies and eating out.	$ 20	
Other	$ 4	

Student page 23

Sample **10. Week 2—Living on Your Own**

Your Paycheck

Make out the paycheck from your employer for your first week of work.

(a) Write in today's date.
(b) The check is payable to you.
(c) What is your weekly take-home pay? (Check your job description.) Write the amount in numbers and then in words.
(d) Sign your employer's name to the check. (Check your job description.)

CHECK NO. 01

Oct 3 20 01 71-587/749

PAY TO THE ORDER OF Lee West $ 225.–

Two hundred twenty-five and 00/100 DOLLARS

FIRST NATIONAL BANK

MEMO Shawn Ducharme

⑆074905872⑆ 251⑈372⑈8⑈ 4311

Your Check Register

Deposit all but $50 of this first paycheck in your checking account.

(a) Write the date.
(b) Write the amount of your deposit.
(c) Write the total amount in your checking account under "balance."

RECORD ALL CHARGES OR CREDITS THAT AFFECT YOUR ACCOUNT

NUMBER	DATE	DESCRIPTION OF TRANSACTION	PAYMENT/DEBIT (−)	√ T	FEE (IF ANY)	DEPOSIT/CREDIT (+)	BALANCE $
	Oct 3	Deposit				175 –	175 –

(continued)

Student page 24

Sample **10. Week 2—Living on Your Own** *(continued)*

Your Savings Account

Deposit $50 in your savings account.

(a) Write the date.
(b) Write the amount of deposit.
(c) Write the balance in the account.

Date	Withdrawal	Deposit	Interest	Balance
Oct 3		50.–		50.–

Your Time Card

Fill out a time card for your second week of work.

Employee: Lee West	
Day	Hours
Monday	
Tuesday	8
Wednesday	8
Thursday	8
Friday	8
Saturday	8
Sunday	
TOTAL:	40

Part 4: Traveling in Rivertown and Walchville

Part 4: Traveling in Rivertown and Walchville

Objectives

- Students will learn to use the bus schedule and route maps to get around town on the bus.
- Students will complete the third week of the *Living on Your Own* simulation.

Materials Needed

Bus Route Map (workbook pages 26 and 27; teacher book pages 50 and 51)

Daily Bus Schedule (workbook page 28; teacher book page 52)

Activity 11: Get Where You Are Going on the Bus

Activity 12: Week 3—Living on Your Own

Pre-teaching

Be sure students understand these words related to the general topic of traveling by bus: *deposit, fare, farebox, board, transfers, request, schedule, route, outbound, inbound, via, departs,* and *arrives.*

Consider reinforcing understanding of banking vocabulary introduced in Part 3, either before using Activity 12 or while going through it with the class. Challenging terms include *register, balance, transcription, debt, deposit, credit, withdrawal,* and *interest.*

Commentary: Introduction

You have a job and you will soon be finding an apartment. There are lots of things you will want to do, but you do not have a car. How are you going to get around?

You could walk—but some of the distances might be quite long.

You could ride a bicycle—but what will you do in bad weather?

You could take a taxi—but that can get expensive.

You could try to get rides with friends—but that is not always reliable.

How about public transportation? In Rivertown and Walchville, that means taking a bus.

Commentary: Bus Routes

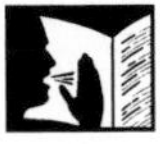

The bus routes in Rivertown and Walchville are shown on the map on pages 26 and 27. Look at the map to see the routes. How many different routes are shown?

Three

Where do they all start?

At the bus station across from Central Park

Describe the different routes.

The Walchville route goes down Brackett Street, along the Rivertown side of the Walch River on St. John Street. Then it crosses on the Walch River Bridge, goes on Anchor Street to City College, where it turns left onto Third Avenue. At David Street, the bus turns right and continues to Dearborn Street and then along the Walchville side of the Walch River on River Drive, across the Veteran's Bridge, and up Brackett Street to the bus station.

The Rivertown Mall route goes down Deering Avenue to Brighton Avenue and then along Thomas Street to Holly Avenue and by the Rivertown Mall. It turns on Congress Street and then onto Eliot Street. At Danforth Street the bus turns left and then onto Deering Avenue and back to the station.

The Congress Street route heads just a little way up Deering Avenue, then east on Congress Street, turning right onto High Street, then along Commercial Street to Hudson and then onto Free Street. The bus rejoins High Street to Park Avenue, Coyle Street, Clifton Street, Longfellow Street, Maple Street, Ann Street, and then takes Congress Street and Deering Avenue back to the bus station.

Commentary: Daily Bus Schedule

A timetable will help you find out what time the buses run and how often they travel the route.

Look at the daily bus schedule on page 28.

A timetable is given for each route.

Look at the timetable for the Rivertown Mall route.

The first column tells what time the bus leaves the station. The second column tells when it gets to the mall. And the third column tells when the bus gets back to the station.

When does the first bus leave the station?

6:40 A.M.

When does that first bus get back to the station?

7:10 A.M.

How long does it take to travel the whole route?

One-half hour

The first bus left at 6:40. When does the second bus leave?

7:10

And the third bus?

7:40

Do they always leave one-half hour apart?

No; the next bus leaves at 7:55—in 15 minutes.

When does the schedule return to buses leaving every half hour?

At 8:40; the next bus is not until 9:10.

Why do the buses run more frequently between 7:30 and 9:00?

Because that is the time when most people are going to work.

Are there other times when the buses run more frequently than every half hour?

Yes—in the early evening when most people would be coming home from work.

Look at the Walchville route. What time does the first bus leave the station?

7:00 A.M.

What time does it get back to the station?

7:40 A.M.

So how long does it take to go the entire route?

40 minutes

Commentary: Activity 11: Get Where You Are Going on the Bus

Activity 11: Get Where You Are Going on the Bus asks questions that you can answer by referring to the bus route map and bus schedule. Questions 8 through 10 ask specific questions about people who use the bus to get to work each day.

Commentary: Activity 12: Week 3—Living on Your Own

Turn to page 30 for Activity 12: Week 3—Living on Your Own. You will be doing pretty much what you did last week:

- Fill out your paycheck.
- Make a deposit in your checking account.
- Make a deposit in your savings account.
- Complete a time card for your third week of work.

But next week you will start spending money—you are going to be finding a place to live on your own!

Evaluation

Check student progress and understanding by reviewing completed workbook pages. Ask questions like these, using some to help students understand how they can apply their developing skills to their own lives.

- What are some good reasons for using public transportation such as buses?
- What are some good reasons for having your own car?
- People who have their own cars sometimes take city buses. Why?
- Do you think Rivertown and Walchville have a good bus system?
- Does our own area have a good bus system?

Extension Activities

Get schedules and other printed information about your local public transportation system, or ask students to do so. Have class members make up questions to ask each other about getting from one spot to another. If your local system offers such things as weekly and monthly passes, help your class do the math to see how much money travelers can save by using them. Have students use the Internet to find out about public transportation in their own community or other areas that interest them. If the class feels that local public transportation is inadequate, ask what they can do about it. Consider having students write letters to the editor or call local leaders to ask for a change.

Bus Route Map

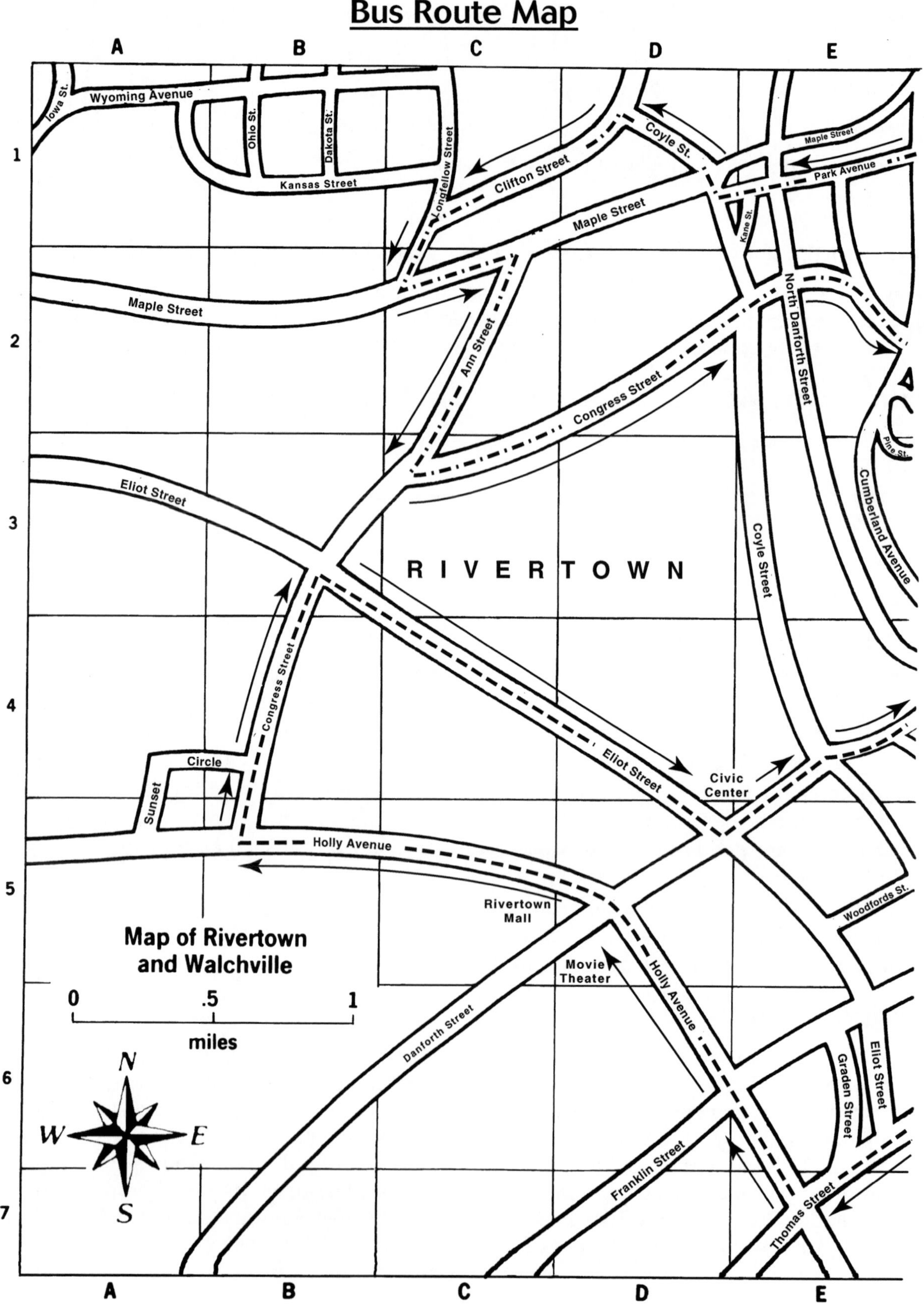

Bus Route Map

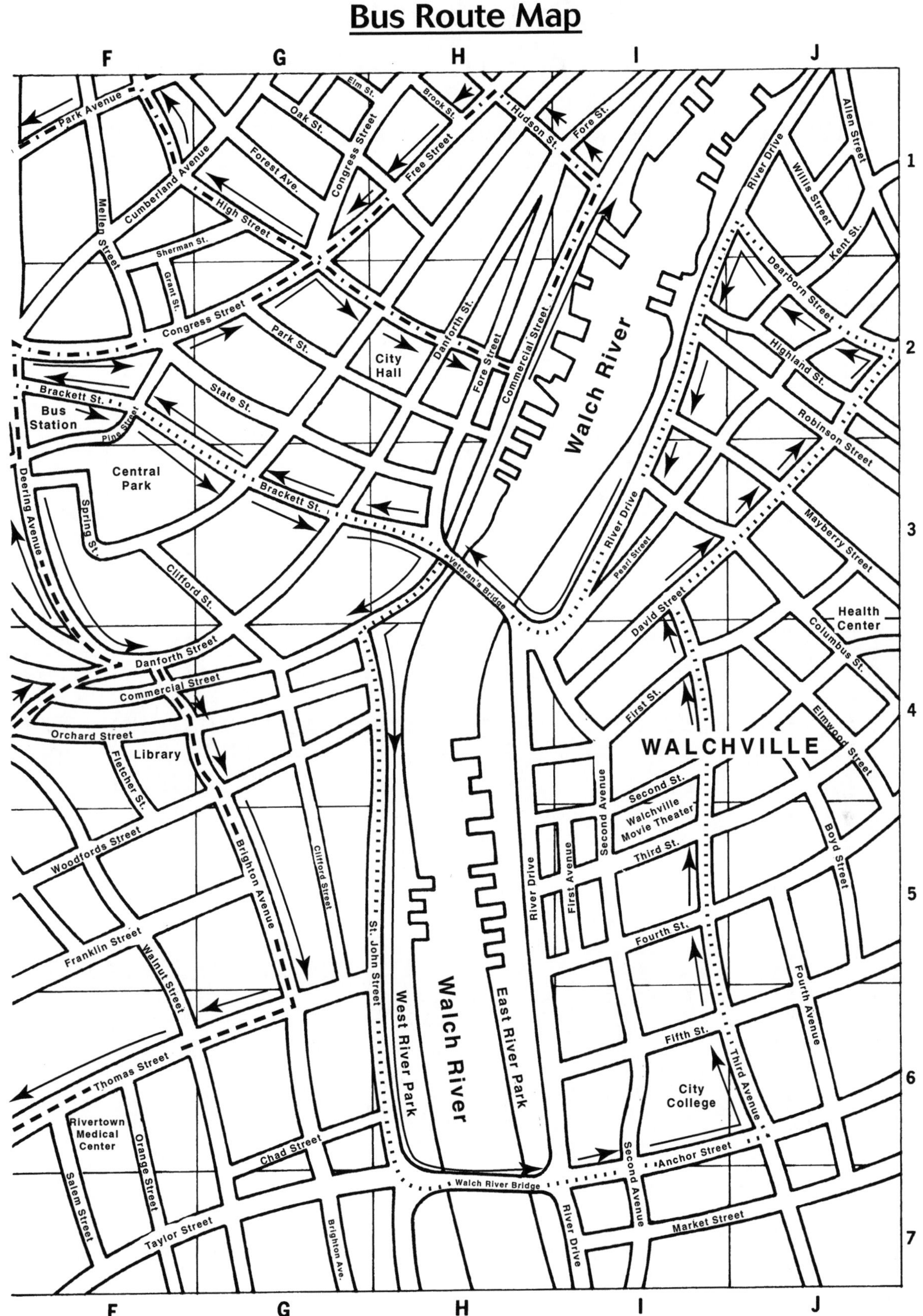

Daily Bus Schedule

- Fare is $1.50 exact change. Deposit fare in farebox when you board.
- Operators do not make change.
- Transfers free upon request when you pay fare.

Rivertown Mall Route (— — —)			Walchville Route (· · · · · · · ·)			Congress Street Route (· — · —)		
Outbound via Thomas St. Inbound via Eliot St.			Outbound via Walch River Bridge Inbound via Veteran's Bridge			Outbound via Commercial St. Inbound via Clifton St.		
Departs Central Park Bus Station	Arrives/ Departs Rivertown Mall	Arrives Central Park Bus Station	Departs Central Park Bus Station	Arrives/ Departs City College	Arrives Central Park Bus Station	Departs Central Park Bus Station	Arrives/ Departs Park Ave. & High St.	Arrives Central Park Bus Station
6:40 AM	6:52	7:10	7:00 AM	7:10	7:40	6:45 AM	7:02	7:15
7:10	7:22	7:40	7:40	7:55	8:20	7:15	7:32	7:45
7:40	7:52	8:10	8:00	8:15	8:40	7:45	8:02	8:15
7:55	8:07	8:25	8:20	8:35	9:00	8:00	8:17	8:30
8:10	8:22	8:40	8:40	8:55	9:20	8:15	8:32	8:45
8:25	8:37	8:55	9:00	9:15	9:40	8:30	8:47	9:00
8:40	8:52	9:10	9:20	9:35	10:00	8:45	9:02	9:15
9:10	9:22	9:40	9:40	9:55	10:20	9:15	9:32	9:45
9:40	9:52	10:10	10:00	10:15	10:40	9:45	10:02	10:15
10:10	10:22	10:40	10:20	10:35	11:00	10:15	10:32	10:45
10:40	10:52	11:10	10:40	10:55	11:20	10:45	11:02	11:15
11:10	11:22	11:40	11:00	11:15	11:40	11:15	11:32	11:45
11:40	11:52	12:10	11:20	11:35	12:00	11:45	12:02	12:15
12:10 PM	12:22	12:40	11:40	11:55	12:20	12:15 PM	12:32	12:45
12:40	12:52	1:10	12:00 NOON	12:15	12:40	12:45	1:02	1:15
1:10	1:22	1:40	12:20	12:35	1:00	1:15	1:32	1:45
1:40	1:52	2:10	12:40	12:55	1:20	1:45	2:02	2:15
2:10	2:22	2:40	1:00	1:15	1:40	2:15	2:32	2:45
2:40	2:52	3:10	1:20	1:35	2:00	2:45	3:02	3:15
3:10	3:22	3:40	1:40	1:55	2:20	3:15	3:32	3:45
3:40	3:52	4:10	2:00	2:15	2:40	3:45	4:02	4:15
4:10	4:22	4:40	2:20	2:35	3:00	4:15	4:32	4:45
4:40	4:51	5:10	2:40	2:55	3:20	4:45	5:02	5:15
5:10	5:22	5:40	3:00	3:15	3:40	5:00	5:17	5:30
5:25	5:37	5:55	3:20	3:25	4:00	5:15	5:32	5:45
5:40	5:52	6:10	3:40	3:55	4:20	5:30	5:47	6:00
5:55	6:07	6:25	4:00	4:15	4:40	5:45	6:02	6:15
6:10	6:22	6:40	4:20	4:35	5:00	6:15	6:32	6:45
6:40	6:52	7:10	4:40	4:55	5:20	6:45	7:02	7:15
7:10	7:22	7:40	5:00	5:15	5:40	7:15	7:32	7:45
7:40	7:52	8:10	5:20	5:35	6:00	7:45	8:02	8:15
8:10	8:22	8:40	5:40	5:55	6:20	8:15	8:32	8:45
8:40	8:52	9:10	6:00	6:15	6:40	8:45	9:02	9:15
			6:40	6:55	7:20	9:15	9:32	9:45
			7:20	7:35	8:00			
			8:00	8:15	8:40			
			8:40	8:55	9:20			

Student page 29

11. Get Where You Are Going on the Bus

Use the bus schedule and route map to answer the following questions.

1. How much does it cost to ride the bus? $1.50
2. How many different routes do the buses travel? 3
3. What time does the first bus leave the Central Park Bus Station in the morning? 6:40 A.M. Which route does it travel? Rivertown Mall route
4. What time does the last bus arrive back at the Central Park Bus Station in the evening? 9:45 P.M. Which route has it traveled? Congress St.
5. Which route do you take if you want to go to the mall? Rivertown Mall route If the stores open at 10:00 A.M., what time should you leave the Central Park Bus Station so that you arrive at the stores just after they open? 10:10 A.M.
6. Could people working a night shift depend on the bus to get back and forth to work? not if they need to get to work after 9 P.M. or go home before 7 A.M.
7. How can you get a transfer to change from one bus to another? ask the driver when paying the fare What is the charge for a transfer? no charge

Help these people in Rivertown and Walchville travel by bus.

8. Sasha lives near City College in Walchville. The building where she works is a ten-minute walk from the Central Park Bus Station. What time should she catch the bus so that she will be at work by 9 A.M.? 8:15 A.M.
9. Ed lives on Sunset Circle west of the Rivertown Mall. He catches the Rivertown Mall bus a little before noon. At the bus station, he transfers to the 12:15 Congress Street bus and meets a friend at the Walch River near the intersection of Commercial and Hudson streets. By 6 P.M., he is ready to return home. What buses should he take? Congress St. Bus/Rivertown Bus What time will he arrive home? about 7:25 P.M.
10. Krista rides the bus to and from work five times a week. How much does it cost her for transportation each week? $15.00

Student page 30

Sample

12. Week 3—Living on Your Own

Your Paycheck

Make out the paycheck from your employer for your second week of work.

(a) Write in today's date.
(b) The check is payable to you.
(c) What is your weekly take-home pay? Write the amount in numbers and then in words.
(d) Sign your employer's name to the check.

CHECK NO. 02

Oct 10 20 01 71-587/749

PAY TO THE ORDER OF Lee West $ 225.—

Two hundred twenty-five and 00/100 DOLLARS

FIRST NATIONAL BANK

Shawn Ducharme

MEMO

⑆074905872⑆ 251⑈372⑈8⑈ 4311

Your Check Register

(a) Bring your checkbook balance forward from last week. (See Activity 10.)
(b) How much will you put in your savings account? (See Activity 9.) $6
(c) Subtract the amount that goes in your savings account and put the rest in your checking account. Write the date, the amount deposited, and the new balance.

RECORD ALL CHARGES OR CREDITS THAT AFFECT YOUR ACCOUNT

NUMBER	DATE	DESCRIPTION OF TRANSACTION	PAYMENT/DEBIT (−)	√ T	FEE (IF ANY)	DEPOSIT/CREDIT (+)	BALANCE $
		Balance Forward					175 —
	Oct 10	Deposit				219 —	394 —

(continued)

Student page 31

Sample

12. Week 3—Living on Your Own *(continued)*

Your Savings Account

(a) Bring your savings account balance forward from last week. (See Activity 10.)
(b) Write today's date.
(c) Make your deposit. [See (b) under "Your Check Register" on the previous page.]
(d) Write the new balance.

Date	Withdrawal	Deposit	Interest	Balance
				$ 50.—
Oct 10		$ 6.—		$ 56.—

Your Time Card

Fill out a time card for your third week of work.

Employee: Lee West	
Day	Hours
Monday	
Tuesday	8
Wednesday	8
Thursday	8
Friday	8
Saturday	8
Sunday	
TOTAL:	40

Part 5: Choosing a Place to Live

Part 5: Choosing a Place to Live

Objectives

- Students will identify what they are looking for in a place to live.
- Students will define words and phrases used in the classified ads for apartments and rentals.
- Students will select a place to live for the simulation.
- Students will list the advantages and disadvantages of living with roommates.
- Students will complete the fourth week of the simulation.

Materials Needed

Activity 13: Think About a Place to Live

Activity 14: Decode the Classifieds

Activity 15: Life with a Roommate

Activity 16: Checking Out Places to Live

Activity 17: Week 4—Living on Your Own

Classified Ads (workbook page 36; teacher book page 63)

Explanations of Rental Descriptions (teacher book page 64)

Copies of Apartment Descriptions (teacher book pages 65–73)

Pre-teaching

Be sure students understand these words related to the general topic of finding a place to live: *roommates, handicapped, accessibility, prefer, privileges, furnished, furnishings, unfurnished, makeshift, to let, advantages, disadvantages, utilities, scheduling, housekeeping, tenant,* and *landlord.*

Review vocabulary associated with the classified ads either before using them or while going through them with the class. Note that Activity 14: Decode the Classifieds will help you with that process, and decide just when to use it (see suggestions below). Difficult words in the classifieds include (in order of their appearance): *affordable, appliances, references, utilities, security deposit, on-site, storage, renovated, applianced, laundromat, maintenance, spacious, facilities, efficiency, combination, kitchenette, carpeted, privileges, condominium,* and *equipped.*

Commentary: Introduction

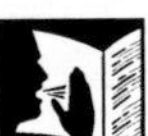

You have a job and some income, so what is the next step in becoming independent?

Having your own place to live!

What are you looking for in a place to live? Do you want a large place? Do you want to be in the city or where there are trees? Do you want to be where you can walk to work? Do you want to live alone or with roommates? What do you want?

Another thing to think about is how much you can afford. A guideline sometimes used in deciding how much to pay for housing is between one-quarter and one-third of your income. If you make $200 a week, how much is that in a month? (Multiply by 4 weeks.)

$800

What is $\frac{1}{4}$ of $800?

$200

What is $\frac{1}{3}$ of $800?

$267

So you might plan to spend between $200 and $267 per month on your housing, and that includes rent and utilities.

What if you have to spend more on your housing just to find a place? If you need to spend half of your income on housing, how much would that be?

$400

That's a lot of your income. Maybe you should think about living with roommates.

Commentary: Activity 13: Think About a Place to Live

Look at Activity 13: Think About a Place to Live. Answer the questions. The last item on the page asks you to describe the place where you would like to live. Try to be realistic, and describe the sort of place that you can afford.

Note: You may want students to consider being "roommates" hunting for an apartment together. If so, consider how to get the partnerships going at this point. To ensure that everybody has a voice in decisions, you might wish to limit group size to two or three. Ask who might wish to be roommates for the simulation, and let them compare their activity page answers before making final decisions. Then let the roommates do some of the remaining activities together, as suggested below.

Commentary: Classified Ads

Open your workbooks to the classified ads for rentals shown on page 36. Look at the main headings on the page. What are they?

Unfurnished Apartments

Furnished Apartments

Rooms

General

What do the headings mean?

Unfurnished Apartments: just bare rooms; the tenant provides furniture

Furnished Apartments: things like beds, chairs, and tables are provided

Rooms: single rooms, usually furnished, often with no kitchen

General: things not covered in other categories; they might include a condominium or a house

Commentary: Activity 14: Decode the Classifieds

Activity 14: Decode the Classifieds will help you make sense of the classified section. The ads aren't always easy to understand. People keep them short to save money, so you have to know what certain words mean. In other words, you have to decode the ads. This activity will help you do that.

At the end of the activity, you are asked to select two places where you might like to live. If you have decided to live with roommates, work with the person or persons you will be living with to select your choices.

Note: The costs of housing vary greatly around the Walch readership area, and there is no way a simulation like this can accurately reflect real prices in all localities. The editors of *Living on Your Own* do not believe, however, that unavoidable price disparities detract from the usefulness of this publication. If the rental rates seem wrong for your area, help students recognize that the simulation process is a good one, but that they need to make adjustments as they apply what they learn to their own community. You might also point out that many young workers just leaving school find that they must share living spaces in order to make ends meet. See also "Adapting This Simulation to Your Own Community," beginning on page *xiii*.

Apartments Students Want to Rent

Note: Each ad in this book and the workbook contains a telephone number. The descriptions on pages 65–73 are arranged in order by phone number—first the 293 numbers (Rivertown) and then the 748 numbers (Walchville). An explanation of the information contained in the apartment descriptions is given on page 64 of the teacher book.

On the chart on the next two pages, write the names of the students interested in each place.

293-1680	
-1784	
-1796	
-2864	
-2910	
-2990	
-3061	
-3465	
-3772	
-3911	
-4119	

-4187	
-4309	
-4920	
-4933	
-5299	
-5623	
-5936	
-6161	
-7741	
-7990	
-8837	
748-0192	
-0293	
-1298	
-2039	
-2917	
-4001	
-4191	
-4296	
-4310	
-4987	
-5192	
-7201	
-7908	
-8318	

Commentary: Housing Descriptions

Note: Ahead of class, make copies of the descriptions for the places each student is interested in. Now pass them out and talk about them.

These are two places you were interested in. Look at the descriptions. Where is each located? Is it heated? Is electricity included in the rent? What can you afford? Which apartment will you choose?

Notes: If neither apartment is acceptable, students can go back to the classified ads and search some more.

For this simulation, it is fine for several students or groups of roommates to select the same apartment. They won't actually be moving in and living on top of each other. Or you can choose to let only one student or group of roommates rent each apartment. The first one gets it; others have to look elsewhere.

Commentary: Activity 15: Life with a Roommate

Living on your own does not necessarily mean living by yourself. You may choose to live with one or more roommates. Like a lot of other decisions, choosing to share an apartment with others has both advantages and disadvantages.

Completing Activity 15: Life with a Roommate will help you look realistically at some things to consider if you have one or more roommates.

Note: If any students in this class have chosen to share an apartment, have them do this activity together and make decisions about things like how they will handle their shared expenses.

Commentary: Activity 16: Checking Out Places to Live

You need to think carefully when you look for a place to live. You need to decide what to ask and what to look for. Activity 16: Checking Out Places to Live can help you do those things. Imagine that you are really looking for a new place to live when you answer its questions.

Commentary: Activity 17: Week 4—Living on Your Own

With this fourth week of the simulation, you will:

- Collect your paycheck.
- Make deposits in your savings account and in your checking account.
- Make out a time card for your work.
- Start writing checks on your account.

And this is only the beginning. In future weeks, you will find there are many other demands on your money when you are living on your own.

Evaluation

Check student progress and understanding by reviewing completed workbook pages. Ask questions like these, using some to help students understand how they can apply their developing skills to their own lives.

- When you are really on your own, do you expect to live with roommates? How many?

- What should you look for when you choose a roommate?
- What are some different kinds of housing? (*apartments, houses, mobile homes, etc.*) What are their advantages and disadvantages? Are apartments best for most people just starting out?
- What kind of furnishings do you need to set up an apartment? How can you get them cheap?
- What are some of the things you need to pay for when you find and move into a new place?

Extension Activities

Bring in ads for local housing or ask students to do so. Go over them in class, and find places that sound good for young people just beginning to live on their own. Discuss good geographic areas to find apartments in your area. Talk about rental and lease agreements. Get samples from local apartment complexes and show them to the class. Use the Internet to look for housing in your area, or ask students to do that and tell the class what they find.

Classified Ads: Places for Rent

UNFURNISHED APARTMENTS

AFFORDABLE
Near Rivertown Mall, quiet second floor, 3 rooms, full bath, heat, hot water, appliances, parking, porch. No pets. References. 293-1796.

APPLICATIONS now being accepted for quiet 2-bedroom apartment, nice neighborhood near mall, $120 weekly plus utilities. Deposit. Call 293-4187.

CITY COLLEGE AREA, 2nd floor, sunny, 3-room apartment. Parking, no pets, security deposit. $400 monthly unheated. 748-1298.

COZY TWO BEDROOM Taylor St., closets galore, stove, refrigerator furnished. No pets. Security deposit $450. 293-7741.

EFFICIENCY APARTMENT. $245 monthly, plus deposit. Appliances included. Call after 5 P.M. 293-6161.

FIRST FLOOR, 2 bedrooms, kitchen, living room, bath, range & refrigerator, Rivertown. Tenants pay utilities. $80 weekly. Call 293-4119.

FOR RENT
Bright, sunny apartment, 153 Pearl St. Call Monday–Friday, 8 to 5. 748-0192.

Maple St., Rivertown. Third floor, spotless, 5 rooms, quiet, stove, refrigerator, heat, hot water, garage. No pets. $575 monthly. Security deposit. Call 293-1680.

FRESHLY PAINTED two-bedroom apartment. $400 per month plus utilities. Call Greg 293-2864.

OAKLEDGE
211 River Drive
Betw. Mayberry & Robinson
- Brand-new
- Two bedroom
- Heated, hot water
- On-site storage
- Swimming pool
- $850 a month

748-5192

ONE-BEDROOM, second floor, 122 Brook St. Includes heat, hot water, stove, refrig., laundry facilities. No pets. $375 monthly. Call 293-8837.

RIVERTOWN
Available immediately. One-bedroom unit in newly renovated downtown area. Wall-to-wall carpet, fully applianced kitchen. $445 monthly plus utilities. Please call 293-5299 for appointment.

RIVERTOWN, 1ST FLOOR, two rooms, heated, parking, security, $350 monthly. 293-3911.

RIVERTOWN, 1 BEDROOM, stove, refrigerator, heat and hot water, $100 weekly. For more information call 293-1784 after 5.

TWO-BEDROOM apartment available immediately near Central Park. $500 per month. Utilities not included. 293-2990.

WALCHVILLE—one-bedroom apartment. Heat included. Tenant laundromat 24-hour maintenance. $500/month, deposit & references required. 748-0293.

WALCHVILLE—one bedroom, $350 plus utilities. 748-2917 after 6 P.M.

32 WOODFORDS ST.—quiet, spacious, sunny, 2-bedroom apartment. Heated, hot water, stove & refrigerator, back porch, shed, laundry facilities, no pets. $200 security deposit. Call 293-3465.

190 ELMWOOD ST., Walchville, one bedroom, 3rd floor, utilities included, $90 weekly. 748-4001 after 5:30.

FURNISHED APARTMENTS

AVAILABLE immediately. Efficiency apartment, heat, hot water, electricity furnished. $90 a week. Call 293-3061.

CENTRALLY LOCATED, clean, quiet, three rooms, no pets, security deposit, call after 4 P.M. 293-4933.

KITCHEN, LIVING ROOM, bedroom, private bathroom. Porch, parking space. 748-2039.

LARGE THREE-BEDROOM, kitchen, dining, living room and shed. Owner pays heat & water. $160 weekly. Call 293-3772 after 6 P.M.

LOVELY LIVING ROOM-bedroom combination, kitchen and bath in Rivertown. $80 weekly, security deposit. 293-4309.

ONE LARGE ROOM, kitchenette and private bath. First floor. All carpeted. $90 weekly. Deposit & references required. 748-8318.

RIVERTOWN—basement efficiency, heat, hot water, electricity, $100 weekly. No pets. For information, call 293-5936.

WALCHVILLE—three rooms fully furnished, bath, heated, utilities furnished. 748-4987.

26 Market St.—one-room efficiency, fully furnished, all utilities included. $90 a week. $150 deposit. 748-4310.

ROOMS

KITCHENETTE, one room, shower, heated, first floor, quiet person. 748-7908.

ROOMS FOR RENT—shared bath, $55 a week. Call 293-7990.

94 ORCHARD STREET, fully furnished rooms with all utilities included. $58 weekly. Deposit. Call 293-2910.

133 KANSAS ST.—one room, all utilities, share bath, $70 weekly. $70 deposit. Call 293-4920.

150 DAVID ST., Walchville, one room, all utilities, share bath, kitchen privileges, $50 a week. $50 deposit. 748-7201

187 Fourth St.—quiet room, $65 weekly, $60 security deposit. Washer/dryer coin operated, refrigerator and cooking privileges. 748-4191.

GENERAL

CONDOMINIUM FOR RENT in quiet building. Fully equipped kitchen, breakfast bar, separate dining area, large living room, 2 bedrooms, 1½ baths. No pets. Lease. $800 monthly. 748-4296.

HOUSE IN RIVERTOWN—six rooms, three bedrooms, two-car garage, large lot. $1,000 monthly. 293-5623.

Explanations of Rental Descriptions

The following nine pages are descriptions of the rental places listed in the classified ads. Below is an explanation of the information contained in each description. See pages 59–61 for instructions on how to prepare and use these descriptions.

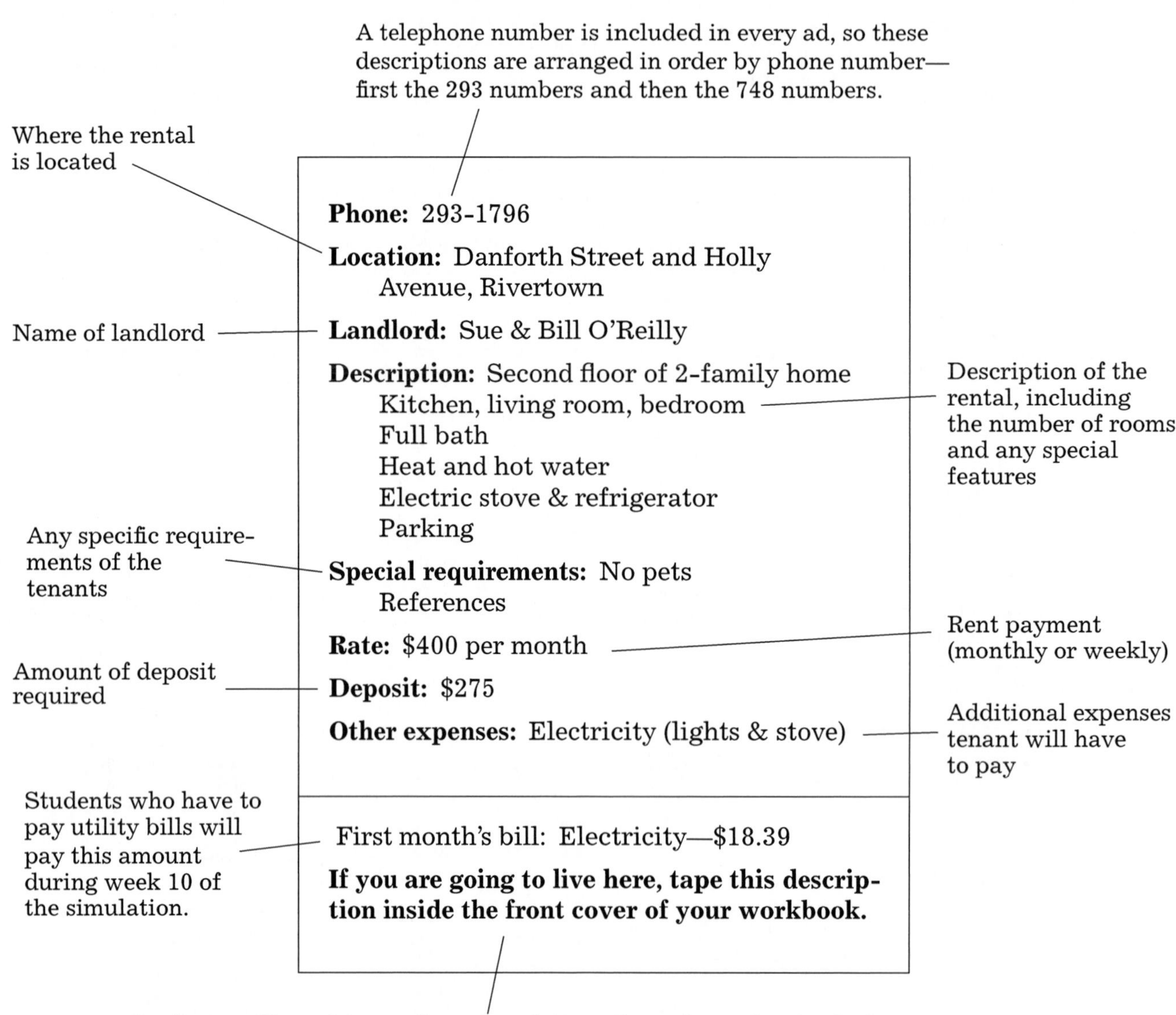

A telephone number is included in every ad, so these descriptions are arranged in order by phone number—first the 293 numbers and then the 748 numbers.
Where the rental is located
Phone: 293-1796
Location: Danforth Street and Holly Avenue, Rivertown
Name of landlord
Landlord: Sue & Bill O'Reilly
Description: Second floor of 2-family home
Kitchen, living room, bedroom
Full bath
Heat and hot water
Electric stove & refrigerator
Parking
Description of the rental, including the number of rooms and any special features
Any specific requirements of the tenants
Special requirements: No pets
References
Rate: $400 per month
Rent payment (monthly or weekly)
Amount of deposit required
Deposit: $275
Other expenses: Electricity (lights & stove)
Additional expenses tenant will have to pay
Students who have to pay utility bills will pay this amount during week 10 of the simulation.
First month's bill: Electricity—$18.39
If you are going to live here, tape this description inside the front cover of your workbook.
Students will need to use these descriptions throughout the simulation. Encourage them to tape their copies inside the front covers of their workbooks so they can locate information easily.

Rental Descriptions

Apartment

Phone: 293-1680

Location: Maple Street & Longfellow Street, Rivertown

Landlord: Joe Lafrance

Description: Third floor
Kitchen, living room, 3 bedrooms
Refrigerator and gas stove included
Heat and hot water
Garage

Special requirements: No pets
Adults preferred

Rate: $575 per month

Deposit: $330

Other expenses: Electricity (lights)

First month's bill: Electricity—$33.50

If you are going to live here, tape this description inside the front cover of your workbook.

Apartment

Phone: 293-1784

Location: Park Avenue and Mellen Street, Rivertown

Landlord: Sam Stanley

Description: Second floor
Large kitchen/living room; bedroom
Heat & hot water
Electric stove and refrigerator

Special requirements: —

Rate: $100 weekly

Deposit: $200

Other expenses: Electricity (lights and stove)

First month's bill: Electricity—$39.28

If you are going to live here, tape this description inside the front cover of your workbook.

Apartment

Phone: 293-1796

Location: Danforth Street and Holly Avenue, Rivertown

Landlord: Sue and Bill O'Reilly

Description: Second floor of 2-family home
Kitchen, living room, bedroom
Full bath
Heat and hot water
Electric stove & refrigerator
Parking

Special requirements: No pets
References

Rate: $400 per month

Deposit: $275

Other expenses: Electricity (lights & stove)

First month's bill: Electricity—$18.39

If you are going to live here, tape this description inside the front cover of your workbook.

Apartment

Phone: 293-2864

Location: Brackett Street and Danforth Street, Rivertown

Landlord: Greg McMillan

Description: Second floor
Freshly painted
Kitchen, living room, 2 bedrooms
Gas heat paid by tenant
Refrigerator and gas stove
Basement storage available

Special requirements: —

Rate: $400 per month plus utilities

Deposit: $300

Other expenses: Gas (heat, stove)
Electricity (lights)

First month's bill: Gas—$14.50
Electricity—$13.25

If you are going to live here, tape this description inside the front cover of your workbook.

Apartment

Phone: 293-2910

Location: 94 Orchard Street, Rivertown
(corner of Clifford St.)

Landlord: Shawn Towers

Description: Second floor
Furnished room
Share bathroom
All utilities included

Special requirements: —

Rate: $58/week

Deposit: $150

Other expenses: —

If you are going to live here, tape this description inside the front cover of your workbook.

Apartment

Phone: 293-2990

Location: Clifford Street and Spring Street,
Rivertown

Landlord: Park Associates

Description: Second floor
Overlooking Central Park
Kitchen, living room, 2 bedrooms
Bathroom with tub and shower
All electric utilities paid by tenant

Special requirements: —

Rate: $500/month plus utilities

Deposit: $400

Other expenses: Electricity (heat, lights, & stove)

First month's bill: Electricity—$38.40

If you are going to live here, tape this description inside the front cover of your workbook.

Apartment

Phone: 293-3061

Location: Clifford Street & Danforth Street,
Rivertown

Landlord: Jed Young

Description: Second floor
Large room with kitchenette
Furnished
Sofa bed
Bath with shower
Heat, hot water, electricity included

Special requirements: —

Rate: $90 per week

Deposit: $200

Other expenses: —

If you are going to live here, tape this description inside the front cover of your workbook.

Apartment

Phone: 293-3465

Location: 32 Woodfords St., Rivertown
(corner of Coyle St.)

Landlord: Martin Brown

Description: First floor
Kitchen, living room, 2 bedrooms
Large bathroom
Refrigerator and gas stove
Back porch & shed
Laundry in basement
Heat & hot water

Special requirements: No pets

Rate: $400/month

Deposit: $200

Other expenses: Gas (stove)
Electricity (lights)

First month's bill: Gas—$14.29
Electricity—$38.50

If you are going to live here, tape this description inside the front cover of your workbook.

Apartment

Phone: 293-3772

Location: Thomas Street and Holly Avenue, Rivertown

Landlord: Ralph Turner

Description: First floor
Kitchen, dining room, living room
3 bedrooms
Furnished
$1\frac{1}{2}$ bathrooms
Electric appliances
Heat & water provided
Shed

Special requirements: —

Rate: $160 weekly

Deposit: $400

Other expenses: Electricity (lights & stove)

First month's bill: Electricity—$41.35

If you are going to live here, tape this description inside the front cover of your workbook.

Apartment

Phone: 293-3911

Location: Clifford Street and Thomas Street, Rivertown

Landlord: Brown Industries

Description: First floor (left front of 12 units)
Kitchen, combined living room & bedroom
Bathroom with shower
Appliances (elec. stove)
Heated
Parking, security

Special requirements: —

Rate: $350/month

Deposit: $275

Other expenses: Electricity (stove and lights)

First month's bill: Electricity—$38.49

If you are going to live here, tape this description inside the front cover of your workbook.

Apartment

Phone: 293-4119

Location: Spring Street and Oak Street, Rivertown

Landlord: Carolyn James

Description: First floor
Kitchen, living room, 2 bedrooms
Full bath
Electric stove and refrigerator
Electric heat paid by tenant

Special requirements: —

Rate: $80/week

Deposit: $150

Other expenses: Electricity (lights, stove, and heat)

First month's bill: Electricity—$61.10

If you are going to live here, tape this description inside the front cover of your workbook.

Apartment

Phone: 293-4187

Location: Franklin Street & Eliot Street, Rivertown

Landlord: George Michaels

Description: First floor rear (of 6-unit building)
Kitchen, living room, 2 bedrooms
Refrigerator, gas stove
Full bathroom
Quiet
Nice neighborhood
Electric heat paid by tenant

Special requirements: —

Rate: $120/week

Deposit: $120

Other expenses: Electricity (lights and heat)
Gas (stove)

First month's bills: Electricity—$63.45
Gas—$19.28

If you are going to live here, tape this description inside the front cover of your workbook.

Apartment

Phone: 293-4309

Location: Woodfords Street and Eliot Street, Rivertown

Landlord: Yana Barrows

Description: Second floor
Kitchen, combination living room/bedroom
Furnished
Bathroom with tub
Heated
Refrigerator & electric stove

Special requirements: —

Rate: $80 weekly

Deposit: $240

Other expenses: Electricity (lights & stove)

First month's bill: Electricity—$40.61

If you are going to live here, tape this description inside the front cover of your workbook.

Apartment

Phone: 293-4920

Location: 133 Kansas Street, Rivertown (corner of Ohio Street)

Landlord: Carrie Jackson

Description: Third floor
Furnished room
Share bath with one other person
All utilities provided

Special requirements: —

Rate: $70/week

Deposit: $70

Other expenses: —

If you are going to live here, tape this description inside the front cover of your workbook.

Apartment

Phone: 293-4933

Location: State Street and Spring Street, Rivertown

Landlord: Alicia Quint

Description: Third floor
Kitchen, living room, bedroom
Furnished
Bathroom with tub
Heat & utilities included

Special requirements: No pets

Rate: $100/week

Deposit: $120

Other expenses: —

If you are going to live here, tape this description inside the front cover of your workbook.

Apartment

Phone: 293-5299

Location: Congress Street and Forest Avenue, Rivertown

Landlord: Jake Oliver

Description: First floor
Kitchen, living room, 1 bedroom
Wall-to-wall carpet
All electric appliances
Oil heat

Special requirements: —

Rate: $445/month plus utilities

Deposit: $445

Other expenses: Electricity (stove and lights)
Oil (heat)

First month's bills: Electricity—$38.90
Oil—$28.75

If you are going to live here, tape this description inside the front cover of your workbook.

Rental Descriptions *(continued)*

House

Phone: 293-5623

Location: Iowa Street, Rivertown

Landlord: Bob Evans

Description: House in suburbs
Kitchen, dining room, living room
3 bedrooms
2 bathrooms
Oil heat paid by tenant
Refrigerator and electric stove
Two-car garage
Nice yard

Special requirements: —

Rate: $1,000/month

Deposit: $1,000

Other expenses: Oil (heat)
Electricity (lights and stove)

First month's bills: Electricity—$40.18
Oil—$28.95

If you are going to live here, tape this description inside the front cover of your workbook.

Apartment

Phone: 293-5936

Location: Salem Street and Taylor Street, Rivertown

Landlord: Luther Cummings

Description: Basement
Large room with kitchenette
Furnished
Bathroom with shower
Heat, hot water, electricity

Special requirements: No pets

Rate: $100 weekly

Deposit: $275

Other expenses: —

If you are going to live here, tape this description inside the front cover of your workbook.

Apartment

Phone: 293-6161

Location: Spring Street & High Street, Rivertown

Landlord: Carter Smith

Description: Third floor
One large room with kitchen alcove
Heat included
Bathroom with shower
Electric stove and refrigerator

Special requirements: —

Rate: $245/monthly

Deposit: $200

Other expenses: Electricity (lights and stove)

First month's bill: Electricity—$37.60

If you are going to live here, tape this description inside the front cover of your workbook.

Apartment

Phone: 293-7741

Location: Taylor Street at intersection with Orange Street, Rivertown

Landlord: Tim Staples

Description: Half of duplex
Kitchen, living room, 2 bedrooms
Heated
Lots of closets
Electric stove and refrigerator

Special requirements: No pets

Rate: $450/month

Deposit: $400

Other expenses: —

If you are going to live here, tape this description inside the front cover of your workbook.

Apartment

Phone: 293-7990

Location: Clifford Street and Woodfords Street, Rivertown

Landlord: Cindy Marshall

Description: Second floor
Furnished room
Shared bath

Special requirements: —

Rate: $55/week

Deposit: $95

Other expenses: —

If you are going to live here, tape this description inside the front cover of your workbook.

Apartment

Phone: 293-8837

Location: 122 Brook Street, Rivertown (corner of Free Street)

Landlord: Frank Purdy

Description: Second floor
Kitchen, living room, bedroom
Heat and hot water provided
Refrigerator and electric stove
Laundry facilities in basement

Special requirements: No pets

Rate: $375 monthly

Deposit: $375

Other expenses: Electricity (stove and lights)

First month's bill: Electricity—$49.75

If you are going to live here, tape this description inside the front cover of your workbook.

Apartment

Phone: 748-0192

Location: 153 Pearl Street, Walchville (corner of Mayberry St.)

Landlord: Martha Betz

Description: Third floor
Living room, kitchen, bedroom
Bathroom with tub
Sunny
All electric

Special requirements: —

Rate: $350/month

Deposit: $350

Other expenses: Electricity (heat, lights, stove)

First month's bill: Electricity—$58.76

If you are going to live here, tape this description inside the front cover of your workbook.

Apartment

Phone: 748-0293

Location: Second Street and Elmwood Street, Walchville

Landlord: Martha Andrews

Description: First floor left (6 units in building)
Living room, kitchen, bedroom
Bath with shower
Electric appliances
Heat included
Coin washer and dryer in basement
24-hr. maintenance

Special requirements: References

Rate: $500

Deposit: $450

Other expenses: Electricity (lights and stove)

First month's bill: Electricity—$39.20

If you are going to live here, tape this description inside the front cover of your workbook.

Apartment

Phone: 748-1298

Location: Market Street and Third Avenue, Walchville

Landlord: Mary Conners

Description: 2nd floor—sunny
Kitchen, living room, bedroom
Bathroom with shower
Electrical appliances
Oil heat paid by tenant
Parking

Special requirements: No pets

Rate: $400/month

Deposit: $400

Other expenses: Electricity (lights & stove)
Oil (heat)

First month's bills: Electricity—$43.05
Oil—$29.68

If you are going to live here, tape this description inside the front cover of your workbook.

Apartment

Phone: 748-2039

Location: Boyd Street & Third Street, Walchville

Landlord: Steve Sample

Description: First floor back
Kitchen, living room, bedroom
Furnished
Private bath
Porch
Parking space
Electric heat and appliances paid by tenant

Special requirements: —

Rate: $425/month

Deposit: $425

Other expenses: Electricity (heat, stove, lights)

First month's bill: Electricity—$58.97

If you are going to live here, tape this description inside the front cover of your workbook.

Apartment

Phone: 748-2917

Location: Highland Street and David Street, Walchville

Landlord: George Plummer

Description: Third floor
Living room, kitchenette, bedroom
Bath with shower
Oil heat paid by tenant
Electric appliances

Special requirements: —

Rate: $350 plus utilities

Deposit: $200

Other expenses: Oil (heat)
Electricity (lights and stove)

First month's bills: Oil—$43.80
Electricity—$37.95

If you are going to live here, tape this description inside the front cover of your workbook.

Apartment

Phone: 748-4001

Location: 190 Elmwood Street, Walchville (corner of Fourth Street)

Landlord: Helen Michaels

Description: Third floor
Kitchenette, living room, bedroom
Bath with shower
Heated
All utilities paid by landlord

Special requirements: —

Rate: $90 weekly

Deposit: $270

Other expenses: —

If you are going to live here, tape this description inside the front cover of your workbook.

Apartment

Phone: 748-4191

Location: 187 Fourth Street, Walchville
(corner of Third Avenue)

Landlord: Sarah Day

Description: Second floor
Quiet furnished room
Private toilet
Shared shower facilities
Coin laundry in basement
Refrigerator & cooking privileges

Special requirements: —

Rate: $65 weekly

Deposit: $60

Other expenses: —

If you are going to live here, tape this description inside the front cover of your workbook.

Condominium

Phone: 748-4296

Location: Highland Street and Kent Street, Walchville

Landlord: Cathy & Bob Lawson

Description: Condominium
Kitchen, dining room,
living room, 2 bedrooms
$1\frac{1}{2}$ baths
All electric—paid by tenant

Special requirements: Adults preferred
No pets
1-year lease

Rate: $800/month

Deposit: $600

Other expenses: Electricity (heat, stove, lights)

First month's bill: Electricity—$81.85

If you are going to live here, tape this description inside the front cover of your workbook.

Apartment

Phone: 748-4310

Location: 26 Market Street, Walchville
(corner of Second Ave.)

Landlord: Amanda Timothy

Description: Third floor
One room with kitchenette
Furnished
Bath with shower
All utilities included

Special requirements: —

Rate: $90/week

Deposit: $150

Other expenses: —

If you are going to live here, tape this description inside the front cover of your workbook.

Apartment

Phone: 748-4987

Location: Anchor Street and Fourth Avenue, Walchville

Landlord: Russell Barrington

Description: Third floor
Kitchen, living room, bedroom
Furnished
Bathroom with tub
Heat and all utilities furnished

Special requirements: —

Rate: $450/month

Deposit: $450

Other expenses: —

If you are going to live here, tape this description inside the front cover of your workbook.

Rental Descriptions *(continued)*

Apartment

Phone: 748-5192

Location: 211 River Drive, Walchville
(between Mayberry Street and
Robinson Street)

Landlord: Oakledge Management Company

Description: First floor
Brand new
Kitchen, living room, 2 bedrooms
Heat and hot water provided
Storage
Swimming pool
Electric appliances

Special requirements: —

Rate: $850/month

Deposit: $800

Other expenses: Electricity (lights, stove)

First month's bill: Electricity—$50.82

If you are going to live here, tape this description inside the front cover of your workbook.

Apartment

Phone: 748-7201

Location: 150 David Street, Walchville
(corner of Robinson St.)

Landlord: Mark Schumacher

Description: Third floor
Small furnished room
All utilities
Share bath
Kitchen privileges

Special requirements: —

Rate: $50/week

Deposit: $50

Other expenses: —

If you are going to live here, tape this description inside the front cover of your workbook.

Apartment

Phone: 748-7908

Location: Robinson Street and Pearl Street,
Walchville

Landlord: MaryLou Matthews

Description: First floor
One room with kitchenette
Furnished
Heat & all utilities provided

Special requirements: Quiet person

Rate: $75/week

Deposit: $150

Other expenses: —

If you are going to live here, tape this description inside the front cover of your workbook.

Apartment

Phone: 748-8318

Location: David Street and Columbus Street,
Walchville

Landlord: Tom Rivers

Description: First floor
Large room with kitchenette
Furnished
Bathroom with shower
All electric appliances
Carpeted

Special requirements: References

Rate: $90 weekly

Deposit: $300

Other expenses: Electricity (heat, lights, stove)

First month's bill: Electricity—$63.19

If you are going to live here, tape this description inside the front cover of your workbook.

Student page 34

Answers will vary

13. Think About a Place to Live

1. How much can you afford? Here's a guideline: between $\frac{1}{4}$ and $\frac{1}{3}$ of your take-home pay. ________
2. Do you want to live alone or with roommates? ________
   If with roommates, how many? ________
3. What is important about the location?
   - Do you want to live close to where you work? ________
   - Do you prefer a city or country location? ________
   - Would you like to be near the bus route? ________
   - Does it matter what floor: 1st? 2nd? 3rd? ________
   - Do you need handicapped accessibility? ________
4. How large do you want your home to be? ________
   - Is one large room enough? ________
   - Do you want a private bathroom? ________
   - Would you prefer sharing a home? ________
   - How many rooms do you want? ________
   - Will you need a full kitchen or are "kitchen privileges" enough? ________

(continued)

Student page 35

Answers will vary

13. Think About a Place to Live *(continued)*

5. What will you do about furnishings?
   - Do you have your own furniture? ________
   - Do you want a place that is furnished? ________
   - Do you want to get by with makeshift furnishings? ________
6. Are there other requirements for where you live? ________
   - Will you get a car and need a parking space? ________
   - Is having a yard important to you? ________
   - Will you want to have a pet? ________
7. Describe the kind of place where you would like to live. ________

Student page 37

14. Decode the Classifieds

Here are some words from classified ads for apartments. Write each word or phrase in front of the correct definition.

lease	security	appliances	references
kitchenette	kitchen privileges	efficiency	tenant
no pets	heated	unheated	deposit
24-hour maintenance	utilities		

(a) no pets — You can't keep dogs, cats, or other pets in the apartment.
(b) references — People who will say that you will be a good tenant.
(c) utilities — Things like electricity, gas, and oil.
(d) deposit — Money a tenant has to pay a landlord before moving in. The money is to pay for damage. If there isn't any, the landlord gives it back when the tenant leaves.
(e) unheated — The tenant will have to pay for heating.
(f) efficiency — Often a one-room apartment with a tiny kitchen.
(g) appliances — Stove, refrigerator.
(h) tenant — The person renting an apartment or a home.
(i) heated — The landlord pays for heat.
(j) security — The main entrance is locked so only residents can get into the building.
(k) 24-hour maintenance — You can call for repairs any time of the day or night.
(l) kitchenette — A small kitchen. It often is not a separate room. It may include a half-size refrigerator, tiny sink, and only one or two stove burners.
(m) kitchen privileges — The tenant doesn't have a kitchen but can use one somewhere else in the building.
(n) lease — The tenant signs an agreement to take responsibility for the apartment for a set time (usually six months or a year).

Look through the ads on the opposite page. Remember what you said on Activity 13, and find two places where you might want to live. If you are going to have roommates, look through the ads with them. Make your decisions together. Write the phone numbers of the two places here:

________ ________

Student page 38

15. Life with a Roommate

Having a roommate can have both advantages and disadvantages. Some advantages are listed on the left. Connect each advantage with a disadvantage listed on the right. The first one is done for you.

Advantages of a Roommate	Disadvantages of a Roommate
1. You can save by sharing expenses, but	your roommate might damage something.
2. It's nice to live with a friend, but	your roommate may not like to cook.
3. You can meet new people, but	you may not get privacy when you want it.
4. By rooming together, you can have a bigger place, but	you may not like your roommate's friends.
5. You can use each other's things, but	your roommate may not pay his or her share of expenses.
6. You can take turns cooking, but	you will have to share with others.

Some Rules for Living Together

How should roommates handle things like rent, food, and cleaning? Write some answers to these questions. *Answers will vary.*

Money: How would you and your roommate(s) pay for rent, food, and utilities? How would you handle the phone bill?	
Scheduling: How will you schedule meals? Will you eat together? How about having friends over? Can anyone stay at the apartment for as long as they want? How about parties?	
Housekeeping: Who does the cleaning and how often? How do you decide what is "clean enough"?	

Student page 39

Answers will vary

16. Checking Out Places to Live

You don't choose a place to live just from an ad. You also go and look at it. Imagine that you are checking out some places that sound good in the ads. What will you look for? Answer these questions.

1. **Safety.** How can you know if an apartment is safe? What are three things to look for?

   ______________ ______________ ______________

2. **Unfurnished.** Imagine that you have your own furniture. What should you think about when you look at a place to live? List two things.

   ______________ ______________

3. **Furnished.** Imagine that you don't have any furniture. You need a furnished apartment. What should you think about when you see it? List two things.

   ______________ ______________

4. **Problems.** You might say "no" to the first apartment you look at. What are three things that might make you do that?

   ______________ ______________ ______________

5. **Questions.** What should you ask a landlord? Write two good questions you should ask.

   ____

   ____

   ____

   ____

   ____

   ____

Student page 40

Sample

17. Week 4—Living on Your Own

Your Paycheck

Make out the paycheck from your employer for your third week of work.

CHECK NO. 03

Oct 17 20 01 71-587/749

PAY TO THE ORDER OF Lee West $ 225.—

Two hundred twenty-five and 00/100 ——— DOLLARS

FIRST NATIONAL BANK

MEMO ______ Shawn Ducharme

⑆074905872⑆ 251⑈372⑈8⑈ 4311

Your Check Register

(a) Bring your checkbook balance forward from last week. (See Activity 12.)
(b) How much will you put in your savings account? $6
    Subtract that amount. Put the rest in your checking account.
(c) Write the date, the amount deposited, and the new balance.

RECORD ALL CHARGES OR CREDITS THAT AFFECT YOUR ACCOUNT

NUMBER	DATE	DESCRIPTION OF TRANSACTION	PAYMENT/DEBIT (−)	√ T	FEE (IF ANY)	DEPOSIT/CREDIT (+)	BALANCE $
		Balance Forward					394 —
	Oct 17	Deposit				219 —	613 —
1	Oct 17	George Plummer (deposit + 1st month's rent)	550 —				63 —

(continued)

Student page 41

Sample

17. Week 4—Living on Your Own *(continued)*

Your Savings Account

(a) Bring your savings account balance forward from last week. (See Activity 12.)
(b) Write today's date.
(c) Make your deposit.
(d) Write the new balance.

Date	Withdrawal	Deposit	Interest	Balance
				$ 56.—
Oct 17		$ 6.—		$ 62.—

Your Time Card

Fill out a time card for your fourth week of work.

Employee: Lee West

Day	Hours
Monday	
Tuesday	8
Wednesday	8
Thursday	8
Friday	8
Saturday	8
Sunday	
TOTAL:	40

(continued)

Student page 42

Sample

17. Week 4—Living on Your Own *(continued)*

Paying for a Place to Live

1. Where is your apartment located? Highland St. & David St., Walchville
2. Who is your landlord? George Plummer
3. Do you have to pay a deposit? yes How much? $200
4. Do you pay rent monthly or weekly? monthly How much? $350
5. Make out the following check to pay your deposit and your first rent payment.
   (a) This is check 1 in your account.
   (b) Write today's date.
   (c) Make the check payable to your landlord.
   (d) Write the amount of the check in numerals and words. (The amount will be the deposit plus your first rent payment.)
   (e) Beside "memo," write what the check is for.
   (f) Sign the check with your name.

CHECK NO. 1

Oct 17 20 01 71-587/749

PAY TO THE ORDER OF George Plummer $ 550.—

Five hundred fifty and 00/100 ——— DOLLARS

FIRST NATIONAL BANK

MEMO deposit & 1st month's rent Lee West

⑆074905872⑆ 251⑈372⑈8⑈ 4311

6. Record this check in your check register on page 40.
   (a) Write the check number.
   (b) Write today's date.
   (c) Under "Description," tell who the check is to and for what.
   (d) Write the amount of the payment.
   (e) Subtract to find the new balance.

Part 6:
Adding Up the Costs

Part 6: Adding Up the Costs

Objectives

- Students will keep track of their out-of-pocket expenses for a week.
- Students will compare long-distance calling rates at different times of day.
- Students will read an electric bill and determine what each part means.
- Students will complete the fifth week of the simulation.

Materials Needed

Activity 18: Out-of-Pocket Expenses

Prices of items as listed on Activity 18

Activity 19: A Week of Your Expenses

Activity 20: In Touch by Phone

Activity 21: Telephone Talk

Activity 22: The Electric Bill

Daily Expenses Descriptions (teacher book pages 83–94)

Box for Daily Expenses Descriptions

Activity 23: Week 5—Living on Your Own

Pre-teaching

Be sure students understand these words related to the general topic of living expenses: *out-of-pocket, expenses,* and *utilities.*

Review vocabulary associated with telephones either before using Activities 20 and 21 or while going through them with the class. Note that Activity 21 is based on vocabulary and will help to build student understanding of it. Difficult terms include (in order of their appearance): *long-distance, full rate, discount, primary, provider, operator, assisted, cellular, dialing, cordless,* and *ID.*

Review vocabulary associated with utilities either before using Activity 22 or while going through it with the class. Difficult terms include (in order of their appearance): *account number, meter number, service period, kilowatt hours, present, previous, presentation, residential, current, average, KWH, usage, rendered, postmark, applied,* and *unpaid balance.*

Review vocabulary associated with daily expenses either before using the Daily Expenses slips or when going through them with the class each week. Most terms are not difficult, but a few that might trouble some students include: *goldfish, vest, aspirin, batteries, wastebasket, amusement park admission, cassette, laundry, handkerchiefs, spool of thread, groceries, donation, stationery, magazine subscription, scarf, gloves, thermos, developing,* and *saucers.*

Commentary: Introduction

You have an apartment and you know you are going to have to pay rent. But what are some of the other expenses you will have living on your own?

Food—toothpaste—bus—clothes—utilities—laundry—snacks—cleaning supplies—etc.

Commentary: Activity 18: Out-of-Pocket Expenses

We have talked about checking accounts and savings accounts, but you will have many times when you will want to pay cash—when you buy a newspaper or a candy bar or a bottle of shampoo, for instance. You will want to carry some cash with you for your out-of-pocket expenses.

Look at Activity 18: Out-of-Pocket Expenses. At the top, sixteen items are listed that might be out-of-pocket expenses. How much would each item cost?

Note: Students will know some of the prices. For others, you may have students go to a store to find a price; have sale flyers or newspaper ads they can look through for prices; tell students what the price might be; or have them make an educated guess.

Now use these prices to figure how much Antonio spent during the week. You may want to use a piece of scrap paper to do your figuring.

Commentary: Activity 19: A Week of Your Expenses

One thing about out-of-pocket expenses is that they can add up very quickly. You can have $20 in your pocket, and then you have less than a dollar and you can't remember anything that you bought. By keeping track of the way you spend money over a week, you will see where the money goes. Then you may want to make some changes in your spending habits.

At the end of a week, total how much you spent on food, on clothes, on fun and entertainment, on transportation, on other things. What were your total expenses? Would you make any changes in the way you spend your pocket money?

Commentary: Activity 20: In Touch by Phone

Talking to someone by phone is a wonderful thing to be able to do. The phone is a great convenience and can be quite inexpensive.

But there is an easy way to make your phone very expensive—and that is by making long-distance calls. Look at the listing of long-distance calls at the top of the activity page. Each call is numbered and specific information is given: the date of the call, the time the call was made, the number of minutes the call lasted, the location called, the number called, the rate period when the call was placed, and the cost of the call. Complete the activity to learn more about the price of long-distance calling.

Note: You might review the chart on Activity 20 with the class to be sure that students understand how to read it and how to calculate percentage discounts.

Commentary: Activity 21: Telephone Talk

Have you ever bought or ordered telephone service? You get a lot of choices, and some of them are confusing. You need to know a lot of telephone terms before you can make decisions. Complete Activity 21: Telephone Talk to learn about some of the vocabulary.

Commentary: Activity 22: The Electric Bill

When you live on your own, you get separate bills for utilities such as gas, electricity, and water. Most utility bills tell you what you have used, how much it costs, what you need to pay the company, and when your payment is due. Electric bills, for example, tell you how many kilowatt hours of electricity you have used. Complete Activity 22 to find out more about electric bills.

Commentary: Activity 23: Week 5—Living on Your Own

Turn to Activity 23: Week 5—Living on Your Own. You will:

- Collect your paycheck.
- Make a deposit in your checking account.
- Make a deposit in your savings account.
- Complete a time card for your fifth week of work.

Commentary: Copies of Daily Expenses Descriptions

In addition, you will start keeping track of out-of-pocket expenses. Do not deposit your entire paycheck in the bank. Save some as cash. Your expenses for each day are listed on slips of paper that you will draw from a box each week. Draw seven slips out of the box, one for each day of the week. List the expenses for each day and determine how much cash is left.

If you run low on cash, you may need to make an additional withdrawal from your checking account. Be sure to record the withdrawal in your check register.

You started writing some checks on your account last week, and this week you may need to write additional checks.

If you are paying rent weekly, you will need to write a check for your rent.

If you want to have a phone, you need to buy one and pay to have the phone company start your service. Make out a check for $25 to Great Phones to pay for the phone. Use another check to cover the service. Make it for $45, payable to The Bells Company.

The description of your apartment (that you attached to the inside front cover of your workbook) will tell you what utilities you need to pay for. To get these utilities hooked up, you will need to pay a deposit. If you need electricity, the deposit is $30 and the check should be made out to the Power and Light Co. If you need gas turned on, the deposit is $25. Make out a check to Rivertown Gas. No deposit needs to be made for oil.

If you are living on your own, you will need to think about the kitchen and the food you will need to prepare your meals. That is what we will be looking at next week.

Evaluation

Check student progress and understanding by reviewing completed workbook pages. Ask questions like these, using some to help students understand how they can apply their developing skills to their own lives.

- Do most people know where their pocket money goes?
- What kinds of things do most people buy with cash?
- How do you decide how much money to put in the bank and how much to keep out? Is it better to have more than you think you will need in your pocket?
- What are some good consumer habits?
- Are most of the telephone extras you can buy really worth the money?

Extension Activities

Have a competition. See who can find the best prices for some of the items listed on Activity 18: Out-of-Pocket Expenses. Bring in some local utility bills for students to examine. Talk about whether utility rates in your area are high, low, or average. Suggest that students with access to the Internet do some research into utility rates in various areas. Talk about what people should do if they think their utility bills are wrong or if they don't understand them. Have students keep track of their own actual expenses for a week.

Daily Expenses

Make two photocopies of this page and each of the next eleven pages. Cut apart the daily expenses and put the slips of paper in a box. Beginning in Week 5 of *Living on Your Own,* students will select seven slips showing daily expenses for each day of the week. Have the students return the slips of paper to the box to be used again the next week.

Expenses

Socks	$ 8.95
Sweater	$18.00

If you went to work by bus today:
Bus fare — $3.00

Expenses

Candles	$ 2.50
Shirt	$13.98

If you went to work by bus today:
Bus fare — $3.00

Expenses

Shoes	$24.50

If you went to work by bus today:
Bus fare — $3.00

Expenses

Bag of popcorn	$ 1.95
Goldfish tank	$17.40

If you went to work by bus today:
Bus fare — $3.00

Expenses

Stamps	$ 5.00
Wallet	$12.95

If you went to work by bus today:
Bus fare — $3.00

Expenses

Jeans	$18.45

If you went to work by bus today:
Bus fare — $3.00

Expenses

Pillows	$14.95
Ice cream cone	$ 2.25

If you went to work by bus today:
Bus fare — $3.00

Expenses

Dinner with a friend	$ 9.45
Concert ticket	$12.00

If you went to work by bus today:
Bus fare — $3.00

Expenses

Candy bar	$ 1.00
Vest	$14.98

If you went to work by bus today:
Bus fare — $3.00

Expenses

Dish drainer	$ 7.50
Dish towels	$ 6.00

If you went to work by bus today:
Bus fare — $3.00

Daily Expenses *(continued)*

Expenses

Soap	$ 1.95
Aspirin	$ 3.15

If you went to work by bus today:
Bus fare — $3.00

Expenses

Newspaper	$ 1.00
Doughnut	$ .95

If you went to work by bus today:
Bus fare — $3.00

Expenses

Movie	$ 7.50

If you went to work by bus today:
Bus fare — $3.00

Expenses

Cup of coffee	$ 1.50
Magazine	$ 2.00

If you went to work by bus today:
Bus fare — $3.00

Expenses

Batteries	$ 3.35
Newspaper	$ .50

If you went to work by bus today:
Bus fare — $3.00

Expenses

Box of cereal	$ 3.49
Milk	$ 1.25

If you went to work by bus today:
Bus fare — $3.00

Expenses

Lightbulbs	$ 3.98

If you went to work by bus today:
Bus fare — $3.00

Expenses

Video rental	$ 3.00
Box of cookies	$ 2.59

If you went to work by bus today:
Bus fare — $3.00

Expenses

Scissors	$ 4.50
Apple	$ .39

If you went to work by bus today:
Bus fare — $3.00

Expenses

Stamps	$ 5.00

If you went to work by bus today:
Bus fare — $3.00

Daily Expenses *(continued)*

Expenses

Ring	$24.48
Newspaper	$ .50

If you went to work by bus today:
Bus fare — $3.00

Expenses

Belt	$ 8.95

If you went to work by bus today:
Bus fare — $3.00

Expenses

Shampoo	$ 2.49
2 pounds of grapes	$ 2.58

If you went to work by bus today:
Bus fare — $3.00

Expenses

Cup of coffee	$ 1.50
Ice show ticket	$24.00

If you went to work by bus today:
Bus fare — $3.00

Expenses

Wastebasket	$ 7.95
2 oranges	$ 1.50

If you went to work by bus today:
Bus fare — $3.00

Expenses

Sweatshirt	$12.75

If you went to work by bus today:
Bus fare — $3.00

Expenses

Amusement park admission	$12.00
Food at the park	$ 9.80

If you went to work by bus today:
Bus fare — $3.00

Expenses

Cassette tape	$10.75

If you went to work by bus today:
Bus fare — $3.00

Expenses

Toothpaste	$ 2.59
Lunch	$ 5.79

If you went to work by bus today:
Bus fare — $3.00

Expenses

Alarm clock	$ 9.59
Aspirin	$ 2.79

If you went to work by bus today:
Bus fare — $3.00

Expenses

Cup of coffee	$ 1.50
Doughnut	$ 1.00

If you went to work by bus today:
Bus fare — $3.00

Expenses

Laundry—washer	$ 3.00
Laundry—dryer	$ 1.75

If you went to work by bus today:
Bus fare — $3.00

Expenses

Cup of coffee	$ 1.50
Bagel	$ 1.00

If you went to work by bus today:
Bus fare — $3.00

Expenses

Laundry—washer	$ 4.00
Laundry—dryer	$ 1.50

If you went to work by bus today:
Bus fare — $3.00

Expenses

Lunch	$ 3.45
Newspaper	$ .50

If you went to work by bus today:
Bus fare — $3.00

Expenses

Laundry—washer	$ 3.00
Laundry—dryer	$ 1.25

If you went to work by bus today:
Bus fare — $3.00

Expenses

Box of crackers	$ 2.49
Bottle of soda	$ 1.59

If you went to work by bus today:
Bus fare — $3.00

Expenses

Laundry—washer	$ 4.50
Laundry—dryer	$ 1.50

If you went to work by bus today:
Bus fare — $3.00

Expenses

Coffee mug	$ 4.50

If you went to work by bus today:
Bus fare — $3.00

Expenses

Laundry—washer	$ 2.00
Laundry—dryer	$ 1.00

If you went to work by bus today:
Bus fare — $3.00

Daily Expenses *(continued)*

Expenses

Library fine	$ 1.20
Bunch of flowers	$ 9.50

If you went to work by bus today:
Bus fare — $3.00

Expenses

Flashlight	$ 4.68

If you went to work by bus today:
Bus fare — $3.00

Expenses

Donation to Cancer Fund	$ 5.00

If you went to work by bus today:
Bus fare — $3.00

Expenses

Video rental	$ 3.00
Bag of popcorn	$ 1.49

If you went to work by bus today:
Bus fare — $3.00

Expenses

Deodorant	$ 2.29
Hairbrush	$ 3.98

If you went to work by bus today:
Bus fare — $3.00

Expenses

Notebook	$ 2.50
Ruler	$ 1.00

If you went to work by bus today:
Bus fare — $3.00

Expenses

Toothbrush	$ 2.35
Clothes hangers	$ 3.00

If you went to work by bus today:
Bus fare — $3.00

Expenses

Lunch	$ 5.50

If you went to work by bus today:
Bus fare — $3.00

Expenses

Lunch	$ 3.95
Newspaper	$ .55

If you went to work by bus today:
Bus fare — $3.00

Expenses

Toilet paper	$ .89
Dishwashing soap	$ 2.29

If you went to work by bus today:
Bus fare — $3.00

Daily Expenses *(continued)*

Expenses

Pen	$ 1.75
Envelopes	$ 2.24

If you went to work by bus today:
Bus fare — $3.00

Expenses

Stamps	$ 3.00

If you went to work by bus today:
Bus fare — $3.00

Expenses

Apple	$ .50
Band-Aids	$ 2.53

If you went to work by bus today:
Bus fare — $3.00

Expenses

Box of cereal	$ 2.74
Milk	$ 1.19

If you went to work by bus today:
Bus fare — $3.00

Expenses

Ice cream	$ 1.50

If you went to work by bus today:
Bus fare — $3.00

Expenses

Bucket	$ 7.69
Sponges	$ 1.68

If you went to work by bus today:
Bus fare — $3.00

Expenses

Lunch	$ 4.41

If you went to work by bus today:
Bus fare — $3.00

Expenses

Window cleaner	$ 2.57
Paper towels	$ .99

If you went to work by bus today:
Bus fare — $3.00

Expenses

Toothpaste	$ 1.79
Shampoo	$ 2.79

If you went to work by bus today:
Bus fare — $3.00

Expenses

Mail package	$ 2.43

If you went to work by bus today:
Bus fare — $3.00

Daily Expenses *(continued)*

Expenses

Movie ticket	$ 7.50
Popcorn	$ 1.25

If you went to work by bus today:
Bus fare — $3.00

Expenses

Newspaper	$ .50
Soap	$ 1.45

If you went to work by bus today:
Bus fare — $3.00

Expenses

Newspaper	$ .50
Bag of chips	$ .99

If you went to work by bus today:
Bus fare — $3.00

Expenses

Museum admission	$ 5.00

If you went to work by bus today:
Bus fare — $3.00

Expenses

Handkerchiefs	$ 2.25

If you went to work by bus today:
Bus fare — $3.00

Expenses

Magazine	$ 1.95
Candy bar	$ .50

If you went to work by bus today:
Bus fare — $3.00

Expenses

Birthday card	$ 2.25

If you went to work by bus today:
Bus fare — $3.00

Expenses

Sandwich	$ 2.95
Soda	$ 1.00

If you went to work by bus today:
Bus fare — $3.00

Expenses

Camera film	$ 6.25
Doughnut	$ .95

If you went to work by bus today:
Bus fare — $3.00

Expenses

Spool of thread	$ 2.25

If you went to work by bus today:
Bus fare — $3.00

Expenses

Groceries $29.84

If you went to work by bus today:
Bus fare — $3.00

Expenses

Groceries $22.15

If you went to work by bus today:
Bus fare — $3.00

Expenses

Groceries $36.28

If you went to work by bus today:
Bus fare — $3.00

Expenses

Groceries $30.91

If you went to work by bus today:
Bus fare — $3.00

Expenses

Groceries $43.57

If you went to work by bus today:
Bus fare — $3.00

Expenses

Groceries $42.88

If you went to work by bus today:
Bus fare — $3.00

Expenses

Groceries $26.72

If you went to work by bus today:
Bus fare — $3.00

Expenses

Groceries $32.51

If you went to work by bus today:
Bus fare — $3.00

Expenses

Groceries $49.92

If you went to work by bus today:
Bus fare — $3.00

Expenses

Groceries $30.20

If you went to work by bus today:
Bus fare — $3.00

Daily Expenses *(continued)*

Expenses

Groceries	$23.59
Ice cream	$ 1.75

If you went to work by bus today:
Bus fare — $3.00

Expenses

No expenses

If you went to work by bus today:
Bus fare — $3.00

Expenses

Groceries	$27.46
CD	$14.95

If you went to work by bus today:
Bus fare — $3.00

Expenses

No expenses

If you went to work by bus today:
Bus fare — $3.00

Expenses

Groceries	$27.72
Lunch	$ 4.85

If you went to work by bus today:
Bus fare — $3.00

Expenses

No expenses

If you went to work by bus today:
Bus fare — $3.00

Expenses

Groceries	$31.65
Donation to Red Cross	$10.00

If you went to work by bus today:
Bus fare — $3.00

Expenses

No expenses

If you went to work by bus today:
Bus fare — $3.00

Expenses

Groceries	$44.29
Magazine	$ 1.95

If you went to work by bus today:
Bus fare — $3.00

Expenses

No expenses

If you went to work by bus today:
Bus fare — $3.00

Daily Expenses *(continued)*

Expenses No expenses If you went to work by bus today: Bus fare — $3.00	**Expenses** No expenses If you went to work by bus today: Bus fare — $3.00
Expenses No expenses If you went to work by bus today: Bus fare — $3.00	**Expenses** No expenses If you went to work by bus today: Bus fare — $3.00
Expenses No expenses If you went to work by bus today: Bus fare — $3.00	**Expenses** No expenses If you went to work by bus today: Bus fare — $3.00
Expenses No expenses If you went to work by bus today: Bus fare — $3.00	**Expenses** No expenses If you went to work by bus today: Bus fare — $3.00
Expenses No expenses If you went to work by bus today: Bus fare — $3.00	**Expenses** No expenses If you went to work by bus today: Bus fare — $3.00

Daily Expenses *(continued)*

Expenses		**Expenses**	
2 CDs	$23.85	Concert ticket	$20.00
Bag of chips	$ .99	Stationery	$ 3.45
If you went to work by bus today: Bus fare — $3.00		If you went to work by bus today: Bus fare — $3.00	

Expenses		**Expenses**	
Gift for a friend	$15.69	Shirt	$13.86
Book	$ 7.95	Sunglasses	$ 9.45
If you went to work by bus today: Bus fare — $3.00		If you went to work by bus today: Bus fare — $3.00	

Expenses		**Expenses**	
Magazine subscription	$12.98	Shirt	$12.50
Mirror	$ 9.50	Underwear	$ 8.45
If you went to work by bus today: Bus fare — $3.00		If you went to work by bus today: Bus fare — $3.00	

Expenses		**Expenses**	
Lunch with a friend	$ 5.43	Bathing suit	$28.67
Blue jeans	$19.35		
If you went to work by bus today: Bus fare — $3.00		If you went to work by bus today: Bus fare — $3.00	

Expenses		**Expenses**	
Saw	$15.85	Winter hat and scarf	$25.49
Hammer	$ 9.98	Gloves	$ 9.84
If you went to work by bus today: Bus fare — $3.00		If you went to work by bus today: Bus fare — $3.00	

Daily Expenses *(continued)*

Expenses		Expenses	
Dinner with a friend	$15.95	Lawn chair	$23.48
Movie admission	$ 7.50	Thermos	$ 6.39
If you went to work by bus today: Bus fare — $3.00		If you went to work by bus today: Bus fare — $3.00	

Expenses		Expenses	
Bowling	$ 5.50	Developing film	$ 5.69
Towels	$12.95	Picture frame	$14.82
If you went to work by bus today: Bus fare — $3.00		If you went to work by bus today: Bus fare — $3.00	

Expenses		Expenses	
Ticket to ball game	$12.00	Radio	$18.52
Food and souvenirs	$12.46	Stamps	$ 2.00
If you went to work by bus today: Bus fare — $3.00		If you went to work by bus today: Bus fare — $3.00	

Expenses		Expenses	
Bathrobe	$24.95	Plates, cups, saucers	$17.45
		Glasses	$ 8.31
If you went to work by bus today: Bus fare — $3.00		If you went to work by bus today: Bus fare — $3.00	

Expenses		Expenses	
Suitcase	$35.95	Clothes drying rack	$12.50
If you went to work by bus today: Bus fare — $3.00		If you went to work by bus today: Bus fare — $3.00	

Student page 44

Answers will vary

18. Out-of-Pocket Expenses

Find the price of each of the following items. Use your own knowledge, look at ads in the newspaper, or check in a local store.

____________	Bus fare	____________	Ice-cream cone
____________	Bag of chips	____________	Blue jeans
____________	A hamburger	____________	Roll of toilet paper
____________	Movie admission	____________	Candy bar
____________	Bottle of shampoo	____________	Laundromat washer
____________	Can of soda	____________	Laundromat dryer
____________	Newspaper	____________	Bottle of aspirin
____________	Quart of milk	____________	Video rental

Read about Antonio's week.

Monday: Antonio took the bus to and from work. He bought a hamburger and a soda for lunch.

How much did Antonio spend on Monday? ________________

Tuesday: It was a sunny day, so Antonio rode his bicycle to work. On the way home, he stopped for an ice-cream cone and rented a video.

How much did Antonio spend on Tuesday? ________________

Wednesday: Antonio rode the bus to and from work. He skipped lunch and went to the store to buy a new pair of blue jeans. Later in the afternoon, he bought a candy bar.

How much did Antonio spend on Wednesday? ________________

Thursday: Antonio took the bus to work. On coffee break, he bought a bag of potato chips. Getting off the bus on his way home, he stopped at the corner store to buy a roll of toilet paper and a bottle of aspirin.

How much did Antonio spend on Thursday? ________________

(continued)

Student page 45

Answers will vary

18. Out-of-Pocket Expenses *(continued)*

Friday: At lunch, Antonio went out with a friend. He had a hamburger, a bag of chips, and a soda. He took the bus to and from work.

How much did Antonio spend on Friday? ________________

Saturday: In the morning, Antonio did two loads of laundry at the neighborhood laundromat. He took the bus to a friend's home for dinner. His friend drove him home. Antonio walked to the store to get a bottle of shampoo.

How much did Antonio spend on Saturday? ________________

Sunday: Antonio went to church and put $2 in the offering. On the walk home, he bought a newspaper and a quart of milk. In the evening, he went with friends to a movie.

How much did Antonio spend on Sunday? ________________

What were Antonio's total out-of-pocket expenses for the week? ____________

What did Antonio pay for that was very important? List three things.

________________ ________________ ________________

What did Antonio pay for that was not so important? List three things.

________________ ________________ ________________

Student page 46

Answers will vary

19. A Week of Your Expenses

Keep track of your out-of-pocket expenses for a week. Write down everything you buy and how much it costs.

Day	Item	Cost
Monday		
Tuesday		
Wednesday		
Thursday		

(continued)

Student page 47

Answers will vary

19. A Week of Your Expenses *(continued)*

Day	Item	Cost
Friday		
Saturday		
Sunday		

How much did you spend on food? ________________

How much did you spend on clothes? ________________

How much did you spend on fun and entertainment? ________________

How much did you spend on transportation? ________________

How much did you spend on other things? ________________

What were your total out-of-pocket expenses this week? ________________

Student page 48

20. In Touch by Phone

Phone company charges for service stay about the same every month. But you can run up a large phone bill fast by making long-distance calls.

Look at the following listing of long-distance calls:

No	Date		Time	Min	To Place	Area Number	P	Amount
#001	6-21	(Mon)	8:28 PM	9	Landisle ME	701 290-5187	E	1.73
002	6-23	(Wed)	11:42 AM	23	Fielding NJ	934 480-2451	D	5.96
#003	6-26	(Sat)	9:21 AM	9	Landisle ME	701 290-5187	N	1.06
#004	6-29	(Tue)	10:45 AM	5	Westland ME	701 498-2981	D	1.54
#005	7-4	(Sun)	8:08 PM	6	Landisle ME	701 290-6638	E	1.18
006	7-6	(Tue)	8:19 PM	25	Fielding NJ	934 480-2451	E	4.09

#=intra-state call P=rate period code (D—Day, E—Evening, N—Night/Weekend)

1. Which call was the longest call (number of minutes)? 006 on July 6th
2. Which was the most expensive call? 002 on June 23rd

Here's a chart from one long-distance phone company. It shows that there are cheaper times and more expensive times to call.

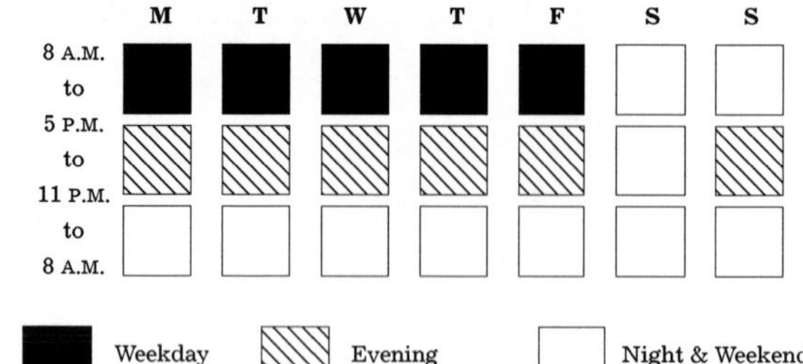

Weekday Full Rate | Evening 35% Discount | Night & Weekend 60% Discount

3. When is the most expensive time to call? M-F, 8 A.M.-5 P.M.
4. When is the cheapest time to call? Saturday all day; 11 P.M.-8 A.M. every night; 8 A.M.-5 P.M. Sunday
5. If a call cost $10 on the weekday full rate, what would it cost to talk for the same amount of time in the evening? $6.50
6. If a call cost $10 on the weekday full rate, what would it cost to talk for the same amount of time on the weekend? $4.00

Student page 49

21. Telephone Talk

When you live on your own, you will probably need to buy a phone. You will also need to pay for phone service. Here are some phone words you need to know about. Write each term in front of the correct definition.

primary long-distance provider	calling card	cordless phone
operator-assisted call	direct distance dialing	caller ID
cellular phone	collect call	
call waiting	basic phone	

(a) cellular phone — A phone you can take wherever you go. A lot of people like them. But everybody doesn't need them.

(b) primary long-distance provider — The company you pay to make most of your long-distance calls.

(c) cordless phone — A phone that has no wires, and you can carry around at home or work.

(d) basic phone — A phone with wires. It stays in one spot, and it often costs less than other kinds.

(e) call waiting — When you are talking on the phone, this service lets you know you have another call.

(f) caller ID — It tells you who is calling before you answer the phone.

(g) calling card — It lets you pay for long-distance calls in advance. Losing it is like losing money.

(h) direct distance dialing — You make a long-distance call by punching in the numbers yourself.

(i) operator-assisted call — An operator helps you make a call for an extra charge.

(j) collect call — You make a long-distance call, and the person at the other end pays.

Look at the list of words again, and answer these two questions:

Which of the phones above is probably cheapest? basic phone

What are two things that not everybody needs? Answers will vary

Student page 50

22. The Electric Bill

Look at the electric bill on page 51.

1. Who is the customer? Clara Reynolds
2. What is the account number? 227-492-018
3. The service period is from June 20, 2002 to July 19, 2002.
4. The total number of kilowatt hours used was 309.
5. The charge for each kilowatt of electricity is $.075 (7 1/2 cents).
6. What is the residential service charge for this month? $23.18
7. How much is past due? $21.45
8. What is the late-payment charge? $ .21
9. How is the late-payment charge determined? If payment is not received within 25 days after postmark date of the bill, a late-payment charge of 1% is added.
10. What is the total amount due? $44.84
11. What number should the customer call for help? 293-0987
12. What was the average cost per day for electricity? $ .74
13. What was the average number of kilowatt hours of electricity used each day this month? 11
14. What was the average number of kilowatt hours of electricity used each day during the same period last year? 12
15. Is Clara Reynolds using more or less electricity this year than last year? Less

(continued)

Student page 51

22. The Electric Bill *(continued)*

Power and Light Co.

Customer: Clara Reynolds
Service at: 27 Maple Street, Rivertown

Account Number: 227-492-018
For information or payment arrangements call: 293-0987

Meter Number	Service Period From MO	From DAY	From YR	To MO	To DAY	To YR	Number of Days	Meter Readings Present	Meter Readings Previous	Kilowatt Hours	Rate
1087	6	20	02	7	19	02	29	22292	21983	309	.075

Bill Due Upon Presentation	Amount
Past Due Amount	21 45
Residential Service	23 18
Late Payment Charge	21
Current Month Average Cost per Day $0.74 — Current Month Total	$ 23 39
Total Amount Due	$ 44 84

KWH Usage	Days	Monthly Use	Per Day
This Year	29	309	11
Last Year	31	380	12

Service bills are due when rendered. If we do not receive payment within 25 days after postmark date of the bill, a late payment charge of 1% will be applied each month on the unpaid balance.

Student page 52

Sample **23. Week 5—Living on Your Own**

Your Paycheck

Make out the paycheck from your employer for your fourth week of work.

CHECK NO. 04

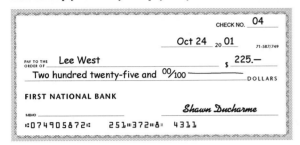

Oct 24 20 01 71-587/749

PAY TO THE ORDER OF Lee West $ 225.—

Two hundred twenty-five and 00/100 DOLLARS

FIRST NATIONAL BANK

MEMO Shawn Ducharme

⑆074905872⑆ 251⑈372⑈8⑈ 4311

Your Check Register

(a) Bring your checkbook balance forward from last week. (See Activity 17.)
(b) How much will you put in your savings account? $6 How much will you keep for out-of-pocket expenses? $50 Deposit the rest in your checking account.
(c) Write the date, the amount deposited, and the new balance.

RECORD ALL CHARGES OR CREDITS THAT AFFECT YOUR ACCOUNT

NUMBER	DATE	DESCRIPTION OF TRANSACTION	PAYMENT/DEBIT (−)	√ T	FEE (IF ANY)	DEPOSIT/CREDIT (+)	BALANCE $
		Balance Forward					63 —
	Oct 24	Deposit				169 —	232 —
2	Oct 24	Great Phones (telephone)	25 —				207 —
3	Oct 24	The Bells Company (phone service start-up)	45 —				162 —
4	Oct 24	Power & Light Co. (elec. deposit)	30 —				132 —
	Oct 29	Cash withdrawal	25 —				107 —

(continued)

Student page 53

Sample **23. Week 5—Living on Your Own** *(continued)*

Your Savings Account

(a) Bring your savings account balance forward from last week. (See Activity 17.)
(b) Write today's date.
(c) Make your deposit.
(d) Write the new balance.

Date	Withdrawal	Deposit	Interest	Balance
				62.—
Oct 24		$ 6.—		68.—

Your Time Card

Fill out a time card for your fifth week of work.

Employee: Lee West	
Day	Hours
Monday	
Tuesday	8
Wednesday	8
Thursday	8
Friday	8
Saturday	8
Sunday	
TOTAL:	40

(continued)

Student page 54

Sample **23. Week 5—Living on Your Own** *(continued)*

Your Out-of-Pocket Expenses

(a) How much cash have you kept out of the bank? That's what you will use for your out-of-pocket expenses. A good amount is $50. If you need more, you can get it from the bank. If you don't use it all, keep less out next week. Write the amount where it says "Cash on hand."
(b) Your expenses for each day are listed on slips of paper in a box. Get seven slips from the box—one for each day of the week.
(c) For Monday, pick one slip and list the expenses for the day. How much of your cash is left at the end of Monday?
(d) Continue through the week. Pick another slip for each day and record the expenses.
(e) If you run low on cash, you may need to make a withdrawal from your checking account. Be sure to record the amount in your check register.

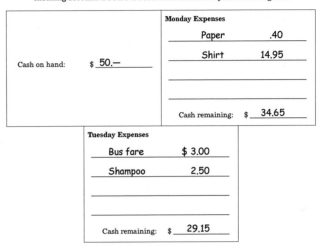

Cash on hand: $ 50.—

Monday Expenses

Paper	.40
Shirt	14.95
Cash remaining:	$ 34.65

Tuesday Expenses

Bus fare	$ 3.00
Shampoo	2.50
Cash remaining:	$ 29.15

(continued)

Student page 55

Sample **23. Week 5—Living on Your Own** *(continued)*

Wednesday Expenses

Bus fare	$ 3.00
Cash remaining:	$ 26.15

Thursday Expenses

Bus fare	$ 3.00
Laundry detergent	2.45
Cash remaining:	$ 20.70

Friday Expenses

Bus fare	$ 3.00
+ Cash	+ 25.—
Groceries	24.19
Cash remaining:	$ 18.51

Saturday Expenses

Bus fare	$ 3.00
Movie	7.50
Bus fare	1.25
Cash remaining:	$ 6.76

Sunday Expenses

Newspaper	.50
Sandwich	2.—
Cash remaining:	$ 4.26

(continued)

Student page 56

Sample **23. Week 5—Living on Your Own** *(continued)*

Your Checking Account

Use the checks below and on the next page as you need them. What checks will you write this week?

(a) If you are paying rent weekly, write a check for that.
(b) Are you getting a phone? If so, make out a $25 check to Great Phones.
(c) Now you need to have the phone company start service. Make out a check for $45 to The Bells Company.
(d) Do you need your electricity connected? The deposit is $30. Make out a check to the Power and Light Co.
(e) Do you need your gas turned on? The deposit is $25. Make out a check to Rivertown Gas.

Be sure to record each check in your check register. There may be more checks than you need. But if not, there are more at the back of the book.

CHECK NO. 2

Oct 24 20 01 71-587/749

PAY TO THE ORDER OF Great Phones $ 25.—

Twenty-five and 00/100 DOLLARS

FIRST NATIONAL BANK

MEMO new phone Lee West

⑆074905872⑆ 251⑈372⑈8⑈ 4311

CHECK NO. 3

Oct 24 20 01 71-587/749

PAY TO THE ORDER OF The Bell Company $ 45.—

Forty-five and 00/100 DOLLARS

FIRST NATIONAL BANK

MEMO deposit for phone service Lee West

⑆074905872⑆ 251⑈372⑈8⑈ 4311

(continued)

Student page 57

Sample **23. Week 5—Living on Your Own** *(continued)*

CHECK NO. 4

Oct 24 20 01 71-587/749

PAY TO THE ORDER OF Power & Light Co. $ 30.—

Thirty and 00/100 DOLLARS

FIRST NATIONAL BANK

MEMO elect. deposit Lee West

⑆074905872⑆ 251⑈372⑈8⑈ 4311

CHECK NO. ______

______ 20____ 71-587/749

PAY TO THE ORDER OF ______ $ ______

______ DOLLARS

FIRST NATIONAL BANK

MEMO ______

⑆074905872⑆ 251⑈372⑈8⑈ 4311

CHECK NO. ______

______ 20____ 71-587/749

PAY TO THE ORDER OF ______ $ ______

______ DOLLARS

FIRST NATIONAL BANK

MEMO ______

⑆074905872⑆ 251⑈372⑈8⑈ 4311

Part 7: Shopping for Food

Part 7: Shopping for Food

Objectives

- Students will choose foods they would purchase to stock their kitchens.
- Students will compare prices at two different grocery stores.
- Students will compile a grocery list of things they need for a specific menu.
- Students will complete the sixth week of the simulation.

Materials Needed

Activity 24: Stock the Kitchen

Activity 25: Comparison Shopping

Smith's Grocery (workbook page 62; teacher book page 105)

Shoppers' Haven (workbook page 63; teacher book page 106)

Activity 26: From the Menu to the Grocery Store

Activity 27: Week 6—Living on Your Own

Pre-teaching

Be sure students understand these words and terms related to the general topic of shopping for food: *stock, staples, perishables, paper goods, comparison shopping,* and *menu.* (See also the commentary for Activity 24: Stock the Kitchen.)

Review vocabulary associated with kitchen staples either before using Activity 24 or while going through it with the class. Difficult terms include (in order of their appearance): *baking powder, baking soda, cream of mushroom, elbow macaroni, granulated sugar, parsley flakes, vanilla extract, yogurt,* and *aluminum foil.*

Review vocabulary associated with comparison shopping either before using Activity 25 or while going through it with the class. You might begin with these section labels, and ask students to identify some items found in each: *Meat, Deli, Oils and Dressings, Fresh Produce, Bakery, Dairy, Frozen Foods, Paper Goods, Cereal/Crackers, Snacks, Pasta & Rice, Beverages, Canned Goods,* and *Baking.* Then, depending on the abilities of your students, you may need to read through the items listed in various sections. One way to make the vocabulary review more interesting is to call out the names of individual items and see how quickly students can find them. If the same student always gets there first, try a different approach. You might try questions like this: "You just found the mayonnaise. Now which item is closer to that—yogurt or rice?"

Review vocabulary associated with menus and grocery stores either before using Activity 26: From the Menu to the Grocery Store or while going through it with the class. Difficult terms include *cookbook, casserole,* and *ingredients.* Other challenging terms also appear on earlier pages.

Commentary: Introduction

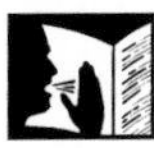

We need to eat to live, but why do we have to cook and bother with a kitchen? There are plenty of good restaurants. Why not just eat out all the time?

It can be expensive to eat in restaurants.

Sometimes you don't have time for a restaurant.

You can have more variety if you eat at home.

You can make foods the way you like them at home.

Commentary: Activity 24: Stock the Kitchen

When you move into an apartment, the kitchen cupboards and the refrigerator are usually empty. Look at the list in this activity to help you decide what you would purchase to stock your kitchen.

There are three different categories on this list. *Staples* will keep for quite a long while on the shelf. *Perishables* will last only a short time and often need refrigeration. *Paper goods* are just what the name says.

Check the items you would want to have in your kitchen. Draw a line through items you would not want to have. At the bottom of the page, list any other items you would want to have on hand. This page will be used with other activities in this section.

Commentary: Activity 25: Comparison Shopping

Most towns and cities have several grocery stores. Why would you choose one over the others?

It could be closer to where you live.

It might have a larger selection.

It could be a cleaner and nicer store.

You might know someone who works there.

It could have better prices.

In this activity, you are going to compare the prices on several items at Smith's Grocery and Shoppers' Haven. Pick twelve items you wanted to buy when you stocked your kitchen in Activity 24. List those items in the column under Groceries on Activity 25. Look at Smith's Grocery on page 62. Find each of the grocery items and how much they cost. Then look at Shoppers' Haven on page 63. How much do the groceries cost there?

Find the total cost of the twelve grocery items at each store and compare.

Note: In general, prices are close at the two stores. Which will look best to students when they shop will depend, of course, on the items they have chosen.

Commentary: Activity 26: From the Menu to the Grocery Store

When you invite guests for dinner, you usually take time to plan the menu and then shop for things you need to prepare your meal. Activity 26: From the Menu to the Grocery Store outlines a meal you might serve to guests and gives two recipes. From this information, determine what materials you already have (see Activity 24: Stock the Kitchen) and make a grocery list of what you will need to buy.

Commentary: Activity 27: Week 6—Living on Your Own

Remember the advantage of a savings account? It pays interest. As of this week, you have had an account long enough to start receiving interest. Ordinarily the bank will do the computing for you, but today you will have to do it. Bring your balance forward from last week (Activity 23). The interest is 4.8% a year, but it has only been a month so we will only be figuring one-twelfth of that. The interest will be determined by multiplying your balance by .004. For example, if you have $80 in your account and you multiply .004 × $80, the interest will be $.32. That may not seem like much, but remember that you have only been saving for one month. If you get that much interest per month for an entire year, it would be $3.84. And that would be pretty good just for putting your money in a bank instead of sticking it under your mattress!

Note: Interest is usually paid only on money deposited for the entire month, not the full current balance. But the above approach is simpler, and some of your students may well be challenged enough by the math it involves to avoid complicating things further. In fact, you may need to pause at this point to review the calculation of interest.

In addition to computing the interest on your savings account, you will:

- Collect your paycheck.
- Make a deposit in your checking account.
- Make a deposit in your savings account.
- Complete a time card for your sixth week of work.
- Keep track of your out-of-pocket expenses.

Next week we will consider the very practical matter of cleaning, so that your apartment is fit to live in.

Evaluation

Check student progress and understanding by reviewing completed workbook pages. Ask questions like these, using some to help students understand how they can apply their developing skills to their own lives.

- How can you save money when shopping for food? (*Watch the ads for specials. Get things in season. Use coupons. Buy small portions of expensive foods, large portions of cheap foods.*)
- What kinds of things do most people buy with cash?
- What if something you want comes in two different sizes? How do you decide which to get? (*One way is to think about unit cost. How much are you paying per ounce or pound? Another question to ask is how fast you will use what you are buying. If you get a large package, will you use it before it starts to spoil?*)
- What are the best food stores in our area? Why?
- What sections in grocery stores usually have the healthiest foods? The most expensive foods? The most fattening foods?

Extension Activities

Have a competition. See who can find the best local prices for some of the items listed in Activity 24: Stock the Kitchen. Bring in some local grocery ads for students to examine. Ask students to create some rules of healthy shopping and eating. (*Find out about the food pyramid and what is good for you. Avoid tobacco, alcohol, and drugs. Watch out for junk food. Read the labels to see what you are getting. Look for foods low in both calories and fat.*)

Smith's Grocery

Meat

Chicken drumsticks	.99/lb.
Chicken thighs	.95/lb.
Chuck steak	2.29/lb.
Ground beef	1.99/lb.

Deli

Sliced cheese	2.99/lb.
Chicken roll	3.59/lb.
Pastrami	4.49/lb.
Turkey roll	4.99/lb.

Oils & Dressing

Vegetable oil	2.50
Italian dressing	.89
French dressing	.95
Black pepper	.85
Ketchup	1.50
Vinegar	.79
Soy sauce	1.15
Mayonnaise	1.99

Fresh Produce

Garlic	.39 ea.
Onions	1.99/lb.
Shallots	.52/lb.
Potatoes	.50/lb.
Lemons	.49/lb.
Apples	.75/lb.
Cantaloupe	.45/lb.
Squash	.89/lb.
Green beans	1.19/lb.
Tomatoes	.95/lb.
Carrots	1.50/lb.

Baking

Granulated sugar	1.30
Brown sugar	.79
Baking powder	1.15
Baking soda	.55
Parsley flakes	1.40
Vanilla extract	1.85
Flour	1.45
Cinnamon	2.05
Honey	2.50

Canned Goods

Peas	.80
Green beans	.69
Corn	.72
Tomato sauce	.40
Tomatoes	.59
Carrots	.75
Cream of mushroom soup	.51
Tomato soup	.35
Tuna fish	.99
Sardines	.87
Chicken soup	.47

Pasta & Rice

Elbow macaroni	.75
Spaghetti	.99
Noodles	.84
Rice	1.50

Beverages

Orange juice	2.00
Grapefruit juice	2.50
Cola	.99
Ginger ale	.89
Coffee	1.99
Tea bags	1.90

Snacks

Pretzels	1.19
Popping corn	.79
Peanut butter	1.45

Cereal/Crackers

Whole-wheat crackers	1.35
Crispy cereal	2.08
Soda crackers	1.20
Bran flakes	1.29
Oatmeal	.79
Corn flakes	1.68

Paper Goods

Waxed paper	1.94
Plastic wrap	1.48
Paper towels	.99
Aluminum foil	1.89
Plastic bags	1.75
Lunch bags	1.50
Garbage bags	2.25
Napkins	1.20

Frozen Foods

Sherbet	1.75/qt.
Orange juice	.99/12oz.
Ice cream	2.69/qt.
Frozen dinners	3.79 ea.
Peas	.89/lb.

Dairy

Cheddar cheese	2.94/lb.
American cheese	2.95/lb.
Brie cheese	5.99/lb.
Yogurt	1.09/16oz.
Margarine	.99/lb.
Butter	2.49/lb.
Cottage cheese	1.59/16oz.
Milk	1.29/qt.
Eggs	1.07/dz.

Bakery

Angel food cakes	1.99
White bread	1.29
Hot dog rolls	1.39
Whole wheat bread	1.35
French bread	1.29

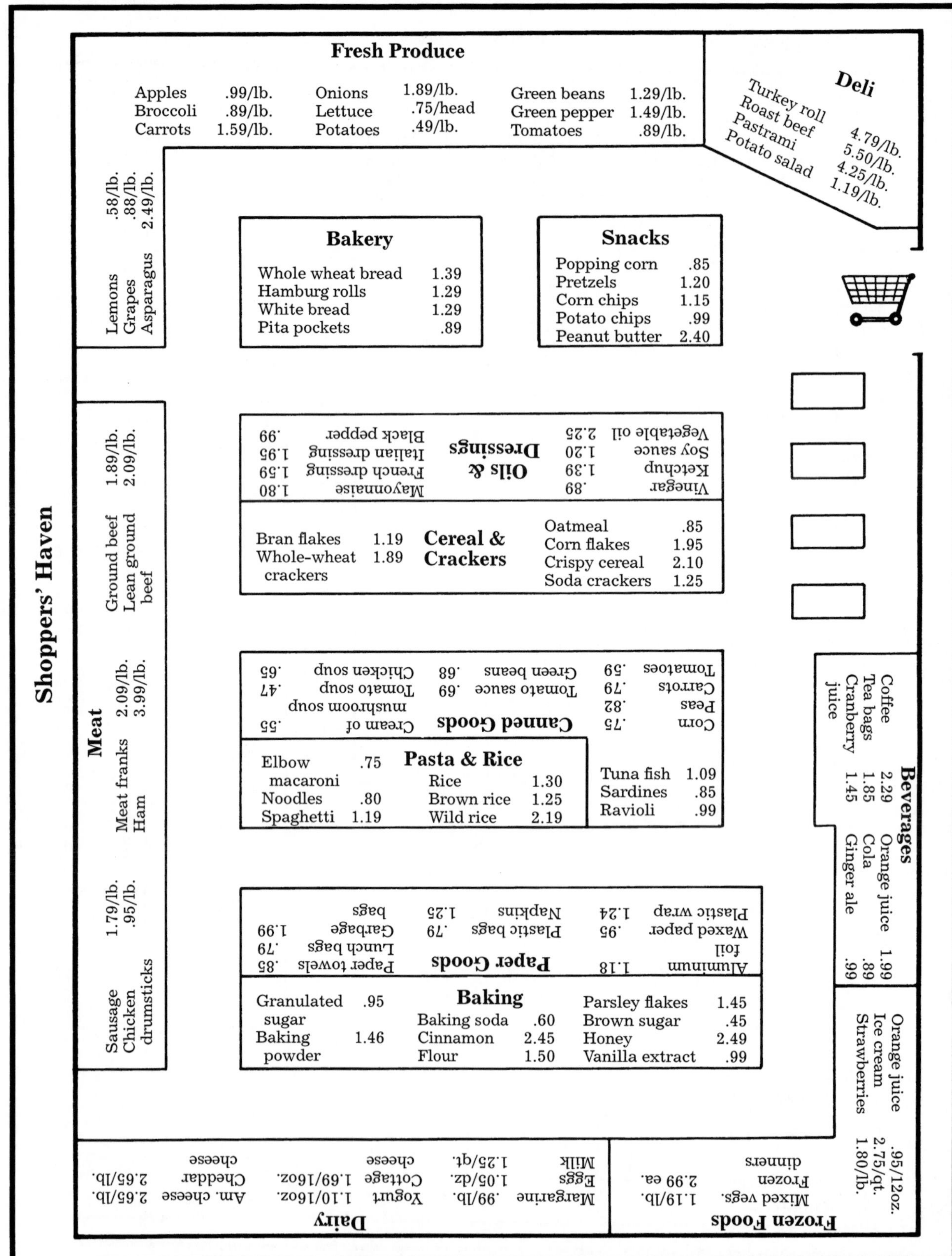
Shoppers' Haven
Fresh Produce
Apples .99/lb.
Broccoli .89/lb.
Carrots 1.59/lb.
Onions 1.89/lb.
Lettuce .75/head
Potatoes .49/lb.
Green beans 1.29/lb.
Green pepper 1.49/lb.
Tomatoes .89/lb.
Lemons .58/lb.
Grapes .88/lb.
Asparagus 2.49/lb.
Deli
Turkey roll 4.79/lb.
Roast beef 5.50/lb.
Pastrami 4.25/lb.
Potato salad 1.19/lb.
Bakery
Whole wheat bread 1.39
Hamburg rolls 1.29
White bread 1.29
Pita pockets .89
Snacks
Popping corn .85
Pretzels 1.20
Corn chips 1.15
Potato chips .99
Peanut butter 2.40
Oils & Dressings
Vinegar .89
Ketchup 1.39
Soy sauce 1.20
Vegetable oil 2.25
Mayonnaise 1.80
French dressing 1.59
Italian dressing 1.95
Black pepper .99
Cereal & Crackers
Bran flakes 1.19
Whole-wheat crackers 1.89
Oatmeal .85
Corn flakes 1.95
Crispy cereal 2.10
Soda crackers 1.25
Meat
Ground beef 1.89/lb.
Lean ground beef 2.09/lb.
Meat franks 2.09/lb.
Ham 3.99/lb.
Sausage 1.79/lb.
Chicken drumsticks .95/lb.
Canned Goods
Corn .75
Peas .82
Carrots .79
Tomatoes .59
Green beans .68
Tomato sauce .69
Cream of mushroom soup .55
Tomato soup .47
Chicken soup .65
Pasta & Rice
Elbow macaroni .75
Noodles .80
Spaghetti 1.19
Rice 1.30
Brown rice 1.25
Wild rice 2.19
Tuna fish 1.09
Sardines .85
Ravioli .99
Beverages
Coffee 2.29
Tea bags 1.85
Cranberry juice 1.45
Orange juice 1.99
Cola .89
Ginger ale .99
Paper Goods
Aluminum foil 1.18
Waxed paper .95
Plastic wrap 1.24
Plastic bags .79
Napkins 1.25
Paper towels .85
Lunch bags .79
Garbage bags 1.99
Baking
Granulated sugar .95
Baking powder 1.46
Baking soda .60
Cinnamon 2.45
Flour 1.50
Parsley flakes 1.45
Brown sugar .45
Honey 2.49
Vanilla extract .99
Orange juice .95/12oz.
Ice cream 2.75/qt.
Strawberries 1.80/lb.
Dairy
Margarine .99/lb.
Eggs 1.05/dz.
Milk 1.25/qt.
Yogurt 1.10/16oz.
Cottage cheese 1.69/16oz.
Am. cheese 2.65/lb.
Cheddar cheese 2.65/lb.
Frozen Foods
Mixed vegs. 1.19/lb.
Frozen dinners 2.99 ea.

Student page 60

Answers will vary

24. Stock the Kitchen

What will you buy to stock your kitchen? Put an X beside items you want to have on hand. Draw a line through items you would not use or buy.

Staples
☐ Baking powder
☐ Baking soda
☐ Black pepper
☐ Brown sugar
☐ Cinnamon
☐ Coffee
☐ Cold cereal
☐ Corn
☐ Crackers
☐ Cream of mushroom soup
☐ Elbow macaroni
☐ Flour
☐ Granulated sugar
☐ Green beans
☐ Honey
☐ Ketchup
☐ Noodles
☐ Oatmeal
☐ Parsley flakes
☐ Peanut butter
☐ Popping corn
☐ Rice
☐ Soy sauce
☐ Spaghetti
☐ Tea bags
☐ Tomato sauce
☐ Tomato soup
☐ Tuna fish
☐ Vanilla extract
☐ Vegetable oil
☐ Vinegar

Perishables
☐ Bread
☐ Cheddar cheese
☐ Cottage cheese
☐ Eggs
☐ Juice
☐ Lemon
☐ Margarine
☐ Mayonnaise
☐ Milk
☐ Onions
☐ Potatoes
☐ Salad dressing
☐ Yogurt

Paper Goods
☐ Aluminum foil
☐ Napkins
☐ Paper towels
☐ Plastic bags
☐ Plastic wrap
☐ Waxed paper

What else do you want to stock in your kitchen? Make a list below.

______ ______ ______
______ ______ ______

Student page 61

Answers will vary

25. Comparison Shopping

1. Select twelve items you want for your kitchen. Choose from the items you checked on Activity 24. List the items below.

Groceries	Price at Smith's Grocery	Price at Shoppers' Haven
1.		
2.		
3.		
4.		
5.		
6.		
7.		
8.		
9.		
10.		
11.		
12.		
TOTAL		

2. Page 62 shows the inside of Smith's Grocery. Search the shelves for the items on your list. Write the price for each item in the correct column above.
3. Page 63 shows the inside of Shoppers' Haven. Find out how much each item on your list would cost at this store.
4. Add to find how much the twelve items on your list would cost
   at Smith's Grocery: ______
   at Shoppers' Haven: ______
5. How do prices compare at the two stores? Are the totals close together? Are prices always less in one store or the other? ______

Student page 64

Answers will vary

26. From the Menu to the Grocery Store

You are having guests for dinner. You will serve them a tuna casserole, a vegetable, and oatmeal cookies.

You go to a cookbook and find recipes for the casserole and cookies. They list the ingredients needed.

Tuna Casserole
8 oz. noodles
1 can cream of mushroom soup
1 can tuna
1 teaspoon parsley flakes
$\frac{1}{4}$ teaspoon black pepper
8–10 crackers
2 tablespoons margarine

Oatmeal Cookies
$\frac{3}{4}$ cup margarine
1 cup brown sugar
$\frac{1}{2}$ cup granulated sugar
1 egg
$\frac{1}{4}$ cup water
1 teaspoon vanilla
1 cup flour
1 teaspoon salt
1 teaspoon cinnamon
$\frac{1}{2}$ teaspoon baking soda
3 cups oatmeal

Now check your cupboards to see what you have on hand. Look at the list in Activity 24 of things you wanted to stock in your kitchen. You will not have to buy these items.

Do you have all that you need for the casserole?

Write the ingredients you need to buy on the grocery list.

Do you have a vegetable you can serve? If not, write that on your grocery list.

Do you have all you need for the cookies?

If not, write the ingredients you need on your grocery list.

Grocery List

Student page 65

27. Week 6—Living on Your Own

Sample

Your Paycheck

Make out the paycheck from your employer for your fifth week of work.

CHECK NO. 05
Oct 31 20 01 71-587/749
PAY TO THE ORDER OF Lee West $ 225.–
Two hundred twenty-five and 00/100 DOLLARS
FIRST NATIONAL BANK
MEMO
Shawn Ducharme
⑆074905872⑆ 251⑈372⑈8⑈ 4311

Your Check Register

(a) Bring your checkbook balance forward from last week. (See Activity 23.)
(b) How much will you put in your savings account? 6 How much will you keep for out-of-pocket expenses? 75 Deposit the rest in your checking account.

RECORD ALL CHARGES OR CREDITS THAT AFFECT YOUR ACCOUNT

NUMBER	DATE	DESCRIPTION OF TRANSACTION	PAYMENT/DEBIT (–)	√ T	FEE (IF ANY) (–)	DEPOSIT/CREDIT (+)	BALANCE $
		Balance Forward					107 –
	Oct 31	Deposit				144 –	251 –

(continued)

Student page 66

Sample **27. Week 6—Living on Your Own** *(continued)*

Your Savings Account

(a) Bring your savings account balance forward from last week. (See Activity 23.)
(b) You started your savings account four weeks ago, so you will get your first interest payment. Write today's date. To find the interest, multiply the balance times .004 ($\frac{1}{2}$% monthly interest). Write the amount under "Interest" and add to find the new balance.
(c) Make this week's deposit and find the new balance.

Date	Withdrawal	Deposit	Interest	Balance
				68.—
Oct 31			.27	68.27
Oct 31		6—		74.27

Your Time Card

Fill out a time card for your sixth week of work.

Employee: Lee West

Day	Hours
Monday	
Tuesday	8
Wednesday	8
Thursday	8
Friday	8
Saturday	8
Sunday	
TOTAL:	40

(continued)

Student page 67

Sample **27. Week 6—Living on Your Own** *(continued)*

Your Out-of-Pocket Expenses

(a) How much cash did you have left at the end of last week? (See Activity 23.)
(b) How much cash have you kept out of the bank to use for your out-of-pocket expenses?
(c) Add these two amounts to find your total cash on hand.
(d) Record your expenses for the week.
(e) If you run low on cash, you may make an additional withdrawal from your checking account.
(f) You might want to use a check instead of cash for groceries or other expensive items.

Cash balance at end of last week (see Activity 24) $ 4.26

Cash from this week's paycheck $ 75.—

Total cash on hand: $ 79.26

Monday Expenses

Bus fare 3.00

Cash remaining: $ 76.26

Tuesday Expenses

Bus fare

Groceries 27.46

CD 14.95

Cash remaining: $ 30.85

(continued)

Student page 68

Sample **27. Week 6—Living on Your Own** *(continued)*

Wednesday Expenses

Bus fare 3.00

Notebook 2.50

Ruler 1.00

Cash remaining: $ 24.35

Thursday Expenses

Bus fare 3.00

Library fine 1.20

Flowers 4.75

Cash remaining: $ 15.40

Friday Expenses

Bus fare 3.00

Cash remaining: $ 12.40

Saturday Expenses

Deodorant 2.29

Hair brush 3.98

Cash remaining: $ 6.13

Sunday Expenses

No expenses

Cash remaining: $ 6.13

(continued)

Student page 69

Sample **27. Week 6—Living on Your Own** *(continued)*

Your Checking Account *Lee West did not write any checks this week.*

Use the checks below and on the next page as you need them. What checks will you write this week?

(a) If you pay rent weekly, write that check.
(b) You might want to use a check instead of cash for groceries or other expensive items.

Be sure to record each check in your check register. There may be more checks than you need. If you need more checks, they are on the next page and at the back of the book.

CHECK NO. ______

______ 20____ 71-587/749

PAY TO THE ORDER OF ______ $ ______

______ DOLLARS

FIRST NATIONAL BANK

MEMO ______

⑆074905872⑆ 251⑈372⑈8⑈ 4311

CHECK NO. ______

______ 20____ 71-587/749

PAY TO THE ORDER OF ______ $ ______

______ DOLLARS

FIRST NATIONAL BANK

MEMO ______

⑆074905872⑆ 251⑈372⑈8⑈ 4311

(continued)

Part 8: Cleaning Up

Part 8: Cleaning Up

Objectives

- Students will identify how often specific housecleaning tasks should be done.
- Students will compare various cleaning supplies and analyze reasons for choosing some over others.
- Students will complete the seventh week of the simulation.

Materials Needed

Activity 28: Keep Your Apartment Clean

Activity 29: Cleaning Supplies

Cleaning products or ads for cleaning products (depending on your approach to Activity 29; see the note on page 112)

Activity 30: Week 7—Living on Your Own

Pre-teaching

Be sure students understand words and terms related to cleaning house. Some in Part 8 that might be challenging include: *housekeeping, stovetop, cupboards, refrigerator, organize, vacuum, dustpan,* and *laundry detergent.*

Commentary: Introduction

Who did the cleaning in your home when you were growing up? Did you help? Well, now it is entirely your responsibility. If the floor in your apartment is dirty, you will have to clean it. When you use dishes, no one else will wash and put them away. They will just stay there and wait for you!

You may like things to be very neat or you may prefer a little clutter. It is up to you.

Commentary: Activity 28: Keep Your Apartment Clean

Look at the list of housecleaning jobs. Some should be done every day, others once a week or once a month. Some can be done every six months or once a year. Decide how often you think each job needs to be done and put a check mark in the appropriate column. If you choose the "other" column, write in how often you think the job should be done.

Commentary: Activity 29: Cleaning Supplies

In order to do your housecleaning, you will need some cleaning supplies. A number of choices are available to you. Why do you select one product over another?

You like the advertising.

You have always used it.

You like what the label says about what it does.

You like the color.

Which of the reasons you have given are the best ones?

Note: The third in the above list is best.

The first part of Activity 29: Cleaning Supplies lists twelve different cleaning supplies you may need to use. Select three of the items. Go to a store to see what your choices are. Then decide which ones you want and why.

Note: Instead of sending students to a store, you might bring in some ads and circulars describing different products. Or you could bring in the products themselves. In that case, pick small and inexpensive items that are sure to be used and not wasted. Paper towels and sponges are good possibilities. Or substitute something else that is not on the list.

Commentary: Activity 30: Week 7—Living on Your Own

Turn to Activity 30: Week 7—Living on Your Own. You will:

- Collect your paycheck.
- Make a deposit in your checking account.
- Make a deposit in your savings account.
- Fill out your time card.
- Keep track of your out-of-pocket expenses.
- Write checks as you need them.

Next week we will talk about another way you can make a purchase—even without money in the bank or cash in your hand. You can charge it!

Evaluation

Check student progress and understanding by reviewing completed workbook pages. Ask questions like these, using some to help students understand how they can apply their developing skills to their own lives.

- Where is the best place to buy cleaning supplies? A mom-and-pop store in your neighborhood? A supermarket? A discount house?
- When should you do your cleaning? (*Picking up as you go helps a lot. So does having a scheduled time each day. Late at night when you are tired is not the best time.*)
- How could you find a cheap vacuum cleaner? (*Look for a used one.*)
- What are some good ways for roommates to divide cleaning chores? (*Start by deciding who likes to do what.*)
- What if you are a neat person and your roommate is messy? What can you do?

Extension Activities

Have a competition. See who can find the best local prices for some of the items listed in Activity 29: Cleaning Supplies. Bring in some magazines like *Consumer Reports* for students to examine. Point out that these magazines can help people get good buys. Anybody who finds them hard to understand should ask for help. Role-play a conflict between two roommates. Use this scenario: *One roommate is angry because the kitchen is a mess and the other roommate promised to clean it. The second roommate complains about having to do so much shopping and cooking. How can they compromise?* Have students meet in small groups to do either or both of these things: *(1) make a list of all the things you will need if you are moving into a small apartment; (2) make a list of all the jobs that roommates in an apartment should share.*

Student page 72

28. Keep Your Apartment Clean

Answers will vary

How often should you clean? You need to do some jobs every day. You can do others once a week or once a month. Look at each job below and decide how often you should do it. Then put a check in the matching column. If you check "other," describe what you mean. Then answer the questions under the chart on page 73.

Sample

	every day	once a week	once a month	other
Kitchen				
Wash dishes	√			
Sweep floor		√		
Mop floor		√		
Wipe off table	√			
Clean stovetop	√			
Clean oven				every few months
Take out garbage		√		
Clean cupboards				once or twice a year
Clean refrigerator			√	
Defrost freezer				every couple of months
Bathroom				
Clean toilet		√		
Clean tub/shower		√		
Clean sink		√		
Mop floor		√		
Wash towels		√		

(continued)

Student page 73

Sample

28. Keep Your Apartment Clean *(continued)*

	every day	once a week	once a month	other
Bedroom				
Wash sheets		√		
Air out blankets			√	
Dust		√		
Clean floor		√		
Organize closets				when needed
Living Room				
Dust		√		
Vacuum		√		
Other				
Clean curtains				twice a year
Wash windows			√	
Wash woodwork				when needed
Vacuum spiderwebs out of corners				when needed

Which of the jobs on pages 72–73 do you like to do most? ____________

Which of the jobs on pages 72–73 do you like to do least? ____________

Are you good at cleaning things now? ____________

If not, will that change when you live on your own? ____________

Student page 74

29. Cleaning Supplies

Here are some cleaning supplies you may want:

broom	dustpan	laundry detergent	sponges
dishpan	paper towels	floor cleaner	mop
dish soap	garbage can	vacuum cleaner	pail

Choose three of these items. Look in a store or at some ads to see what choices are available for these items. What are their advantages and disadvantages? Which ones will you buy? Why?

Answers will vary

Sample

Item 1: Sponges

Possible choices:

large heavy-duty sponge — $2.79 — last a long time — good for cleaning car — not for dishes or cleaning smaller areas

small sponge — $1.29 — hold easily

sponge with scour pad on back — $1.89 — will scrub hard-to-clean area; might be rough on hands

I will buy sponge with scour pad because it's most useful for kitchen cleaning.

Item 2:

Possible choices:

____

I will buy ____________ because ____________.

Item 3:

Possible choices:

____

I will buy ____________ because ____________.

Student page 75

Sample

30. Week 7—Living on Your Own

Your Paycheck

Make out the paycheck from your employer for your sixth week of work.

CHECK NO. 06

Nov. 7 20 01 71-587/749

PAY TO THE ORDER OF Lee West $ 225.—

Two hundred twenty-five and 00/100 DOLLARS

FIRST NATIONAL BANK

MEMO

Shawn Ducharme

⑆074905872⑆ 251⑈372⑈8⑈ 4311

Your Check Register

(a) Bring your checkbook balance forward from last week. (See Activity 27.)

(b) How much will you put in your savings account? 6 How much will you keep for out-of-pocket expenses? 75 Deposit the rest in your checking account.

RECORD ALL CHARGES OR CREDITS THAT AFFECT YOUR ACCOUNT

NUMBER	DATE	DESCRIPTION OF TRANSACTION	PAYMENT/DEBIT (−)	√ T	FEE (IF ANY) (−)	DEPOSIT/CREDIT (+)	BALANCE $
		Balance Forward					251 —
	Nov 7	Deposit				144 —	395 —
5	Nov 12	The Grocery Store	32 76				362 24

(continued)

Student page 76

Sample **30. Week 7—Living on Your Own** *(continued)*

Your Savings Account

(a) Bring your savings account balance forward from last week. (See Activity 27.)
(b) Write today's date.
(c) Make your deposit.
(d) Write the new balance.

Date	Withdrawal	Deposit	Interest	Balance
				74.27
Nov 7		6.—		80.27

Your Time Card

Fill out a time card for your seventh week of work.

Employee: Lee West

Day	Hours
Monday	
Tuesday	8
Wednesday	8
Thursday	8
Friday	8
Saturday	8
Sunday	
TOTAL:	40

(continued)

Student page 77

Sample **30. Week 7—Living on Your Own** *(continued)*

Your Out-of-Pocket Expenses

(a) How much cash did you have left at the end of last week? (See Activity 27.)
(b) How much cash have you kept out of the bank to use for your out-of-pocket expenses?
(c) Add these two amounts to find your total cash on hand.
(d) Record your expenses for the week.
(e) If you run low on cash, you may make an additional withdrawal from your checking account.
(f) You might want to use a check instead of cash for groceries or other expensive items.

Cash balance at end of last week (see Activity 28) $ 6.13

Cash from this week's paycheck $ 75.—

Total cash on hand: $ 81.13

Monday Expenses

Gift for a friend	15.69
Book	7.95

Cash remaining: $ 57.49

Tuesday Expenses

Bus fare	3.00
Toothbrush	2.35

Cash remaining: $ 52.14

(continued)

Student page 78

Sample **30. Week 7—Living on Your Own** *(continued)*

Wednesday Expenses

Bus fare	3.00
Shirt	12.50
New underwear	8.45

Cash remaining: $ 28.19

Thursday Expenses

Bus fare	3.00

Cash remaining: $ 25.19

Friday Expenses

Bus fare	3.00
Groceries (paid by check)	

Cash remaining: $ 22.19

Saturday Expenses

Bus fare	3.00
Lunch	3.50

Cash remaining: $ 15.69

Sunday Expenses

Flashlight	4.68

Cash remaining: $ 11.01

(continued)

Student page 79

Sample **30. Week 7—Living on Your Own** *(continued)*

Your Checking Account

Use the checks below and on the next page as you need them. What checks will you write this week?

(a) If you pay rent weekly, write that check.
(b) You might want to use a check instead of cash for groceries or other expensive items.

Be sure to record each check in your check register. There may be more checks than you need. If you need more checks, they are on the next page and at the back of the book.

CHECK NO. 5

Nov. 12 20 01 71-587/749

PAY TO THE ORDER OF The Grocery Store $ 32.76

Thirty-two and 76/100 DOLLARS

FIRST NATIONAL BANK

MEMO Groceries Lee West

⑆074905872⑆ 251⑈372⑈8⑈ 4311

CHECK NO. ____

____ 20 ____ 71-587/749

PAY TO THE ORDER OF ____ $ ____

____ DOLLARS

FIRST NATIONAL BANK

MEMO ____

⑆074905872⑆ 251⑈372⑈8⑈ 4311

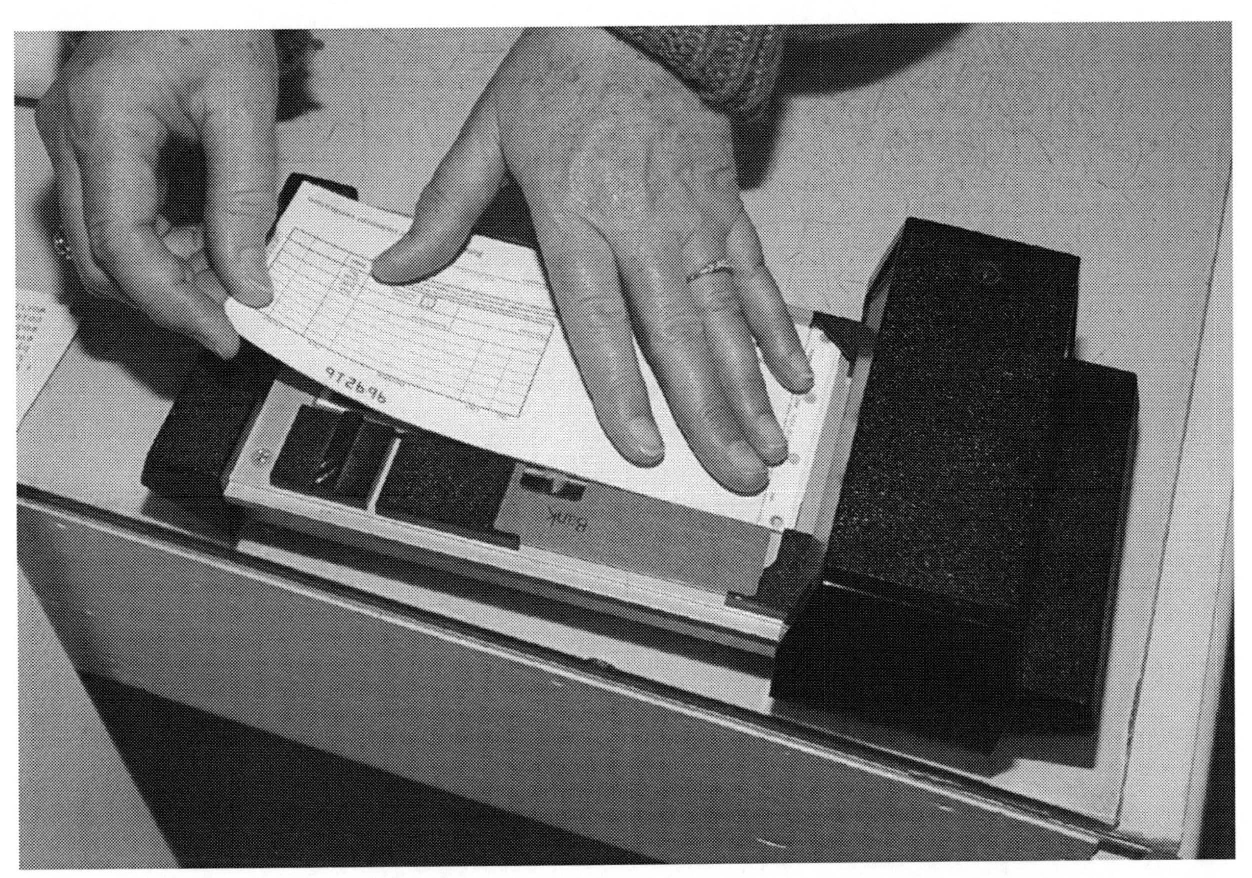

Part 9:
Charging to the Future

Part 9: Charging to the Future

Objectives

- Students will review the various charges on credit-card bills.
- Students will make out a credit-card application.
- Students will complete the eighth week of the simulation.

Materials Needed

Activity 31: Paying After You Charge

Activity 32: Credit-Card Application

Copies of Daily Expenses with Larger Purchases (teacher book pages 123 and 124)

Activity 33: Week 8—Living on Your Own

Pre-teaching

Be sure students understand the general vocabulary of credit. Words and terms in Part 9 include: *credit, charge,* and *statement.*

Review vocabulary related to credit-card statements either before looking at them or while going through Activity 31 with the class. Words and terms include: *credit line, transaction, description of purchase, previous balance, minimum payment due, subject to finance charge, monthly periodic rate,* and *annual percentage rate.*

Review vocabulary related to credit-card applications either before completing them or while going through Activity 32 with the class. Words and terms include: *application, special, approving, hereby, Social Security number, dependents, previous, relative, relationship, position, gross pay, alimony, child support, separate maintenance payments, revealed, consider, evaluating, credit references, debts, credit unions, finance companies, creditworthiness, jointly, living facilities, property, joint, mortgage balance, mortgage holder, establishing, authorize, obtain, desire, undersigned, issue, subject to, conditions, disclosure, said terms and conditions, presumed, subsequent,* and *obtain.*

Commentary: Introduction

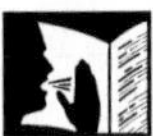

Up until now, you have been buying things two ways—you have either written a check or paid cash. But there is another way to buy things—a way that lets you put off paying the money until later. How do you think you can do that?

With a credit card

What are the good things about a credit card?

It lets you get things when you don't have cash.

You don't have to carry cash.

Many stores accept them.

Using a card puts many different expenses on one bill.

What are some bad things about a charge card?

You can easily spend more money than you have.

If you lose your card, someone else can find it and use it.

Interest is added if you don't pay right away, so you end up paying more for things.

Commentary: Activity 31: Paying After You Charge

Activity 31: Paying After You Charge shows three months of statements for a credit card. Look at the first statement, dated June 25. What purchases were made during June?

A shirt for $15.25

A television for $289.43

What is the total amount due?

$304.68

Why is there no interest?

This is the first statement for charges made that month.

Go on to look at the statement dated July 25. Then answer the questions in the activity. You will be making out the statement for August 25.

Note: The math required for this activity is more rigorous than most required by *Living on Your Own*. The activity page does lead students carefully through the required steps, but you may want to review procedures with your class before assigning the work.

Commentary: Activity 32: Credit-Card Application

Can you just go into any store and charge your purchase?

No. But you can charge in a lot of stores if you have a credit card.

And to get a card, you have to fill out an application. Look at the application in Activity 32: Credit-Card Application. Read it over; then fill out the information requested.

Note: Some students may find this form difficult enough so that you should go through it carefully with the full class.

Commentary: Activity 33: Week 8—Living on Your Own

Beginning this week of the simulation, you will be able to charge purchases greater than $10.00. There is a place near the end of Activity 33 (on page 88 of your workbook) where you can list items that you decide to charge. List each item, the date you bought it, and the cost of the item.

Note: Add these Daily Expenses with Larger Purchases to your box of Daily Expenses. Luck will determine which students draw them and buy large-ticket items. Those who have low expenses and plenty of cash may not charge anything at all.

During the eighth week of the simulation, you will:

- Collect your paycheck.
- Make a deposit in your checking account.
- Make a deposit in your savings account.
- Fill out your time card.
- Keep track of your out-of-pocket expenses.

• Write checks as you need them.

Remember—you can charge some of your more expensive purchases instead of paying with cash or a check. But you will have to pay for them in the future!

Evaluation

Check student progress and understanding by reviewing completed workbook pages. Ask questions like these, using some to help students understand how they can apply their developing skills to their own lives.

- Are credit cards a good idea for young people? (*They are convenient but dangerous for a lot of people of every age.*)
- Have you ever received an offer for credit cards in the mail? (*A lot of people do.*)
- What are some other ways to buy things when you don't have cash? (*Borrowing money; using in-store charge cards and accounts.*)
- What are debit cards? (*When you use them, money comes directly out of your bank account. You don't wait to pay.*)
- What if you charge so much you can't pay? What should you do? (*Talk to the credit-card company. Talk to your bank. Ask a financial counselor for help. Get rid of your credit card.*)

Extension Activities

Talk about the importance of paying bills on time. Ask a banker or a financial counselor to talk with your class about credit cards. Get some actual application forms for students to see. Bring in an actual credit-card statement for students to see. Point out that things often cost more when you charge or borrow for them, and ask when it makes sense to pay the extra money. (*If you need a car or new clothes to take a job; when you have unexpected health needs; etc.*)

32. Credit-Card Application

Bank Use Only	Account Number	Special Instructions					
		Line of Credit	M.C. Cards	Visa Cards	Exp. Date	Approving Officer	Date of Approval

Type of Account Joint ☐ Individual ☐ I hereby apply for ☐ Credit Card

MY LAST NAME (PLEASE PRINT) FIRST NAME (INITIAL)	DATE OF BIRTH	SOCIAL SECURITY NUMBER

HOME ADDRESS (STREET) (CITY) (STATE) (ZIP)	YEARS THERE	DEPENDENTS NO.

HOME PHONE	PREVIOUS ADDRESS (STREET) (CITY) (STATE) (ZIP)	YEARS THERE

NEAREST RELATIVE NOT LIVING WITH ME RELATIVE'S ADDRESS	RELATIONSHIP

I AM EMPLOYED BY (COMPANY) (CITY)	MY POSITION IS	BUSINESS PHONE	YEARS THERE	MONTHLY GROSS PAY $

PREVIOUSLY EMPLOYED BY (COMPANY) (CITY) (STATE)	YEARS THERE	

OTHER INCOME	INCOME FROM ALIMONY, CHILD SUPPORT, OR SEPARATE MAINTENANCE PAYMENTS NEED NOT BE REVEALED IF YOU DON'T WANT US TO CONSIDER IT IN EVALUATING YOUR APPLICATION	SOURCE	AMOUNT	OTHER MONTHLY INCOME $

MY LAST NAME (PLEASE PRINT) FIRST NAME (INITIAL)	SOCIAL SECURITY NUMBER	DATE OF BIRTH

HOME ADDRESS (STREET) (CITY) (STATE) (ZIP)	YEARS THERE	DEPENDENTS NO.

HOME PHONE	PREVIOUS ADDRESS (STREET) (CITY) (STATE) (ZIP)	YEARS THERE

NEAREST RELATIVE NOT LIVING WITH ME RELATIVE'S ADDRESS	RELATIONSHIP

I AM EMPLOYED BY (COMPANY) (CITY)	MY POSITION IS	BUSINESS PHONE	YEARS THERE	MONTHLY GROSS PAY $

PREVIOUSLY EMPLOYED BY (COMPANY) (CITY) (STATE)	YEARS THERE	

OTHER INCOME	INCOME FROM ALIMONY, CHILD SUPPORT, OR SEPARATE MAINTENANCE PAYMENTS NEED NOT BE REVEALED IF YOU DON'T WANT US TO CONSIDER IT IN EVALUATING YOUR APPLICATION	SOURCE	AMOUNT	OTHER MONTHLY INCOME $

CREDIT REFERENCES (LIST OPEN OR CLOSED ACCOUNTS)

List debts owed to banks, credit unions, finance companies, credit card and department store credit plans, etc.
If you are applying for credit individually and are not relying on the credit worthiness of another person, list only the debts owed by you or you and another person jointly. Please use another page to list additional references if necessary.

Checking Account Bank/Account Number	Savings Account Bank/Account Number	Other Types of Deposits/Account Number

COMPANY AND ADDRESS	ORIGINAL AMOUNT	UNPAID AMOUNT	ACCOUNT NO.	MONTHLY PAYMENT
	$	$		$
	$	$		$
	$	$		$
AUTO LOAN	AUTO MAKE & MODEL	$		$

MY LIVING FACILITIES ARE ☐ RENTED ☐ OWNED ☐ I LIVE WITH RELATIVES	MY PROPERTY IS IN ☐ MY NAME ONLY ☐ JOINT	PRESENT VALUE $	PURCHASE PRICE $	MORTGAGE BALANCE $	AMOUNT OF MY MONTHLY PAYMENT	$

NAME AND ADDRESS OF MY LANDLORD OR MORTGAGE HOLDER IS	TOTAL OF ALL MONTHLY PAYMENTS	$

I/We certify that the above information is true and correct and is given for the purpose of establishing a Credit Card Account. I/We hereby authorize you to obtain any such information as you may desire relative to this application from any source. The Undersigned hereby applies to the Credit Card Servicing Center to establish a Credit Card Account in the name of the Undersigned and further requests The Credit Card Servicing Center to issue to Undersigned Credit Cards subject to the terms and conditions of the Credit Card Disclosure Statement which will be sent to Undersigned upon approval of this application by The Credit Card Servicing Center. Undersigned understands that acceptance of said terms and conditions may be in writing or may be presumed from subsequent use of the account to obtain credit.

X ______________________ X ______________________ ________

Signature of 1st Card Holder Applicant — Other Signature if Joint Account — Date

Daily Expenses with Larger Purchases

Photocopy this and the next page. Cut apart the slips and add them to the box containing Daily Expenses for week 5 and the rest of the simulation. These include some larger purchases. Students who draw these may wish to charge their larger purchases.

Expenses

Videocassette recorder	$278.00
Rental on two videos	$ 6.00

If you went to work by bus today:
Bus fare — $3.00

Expenses

Living room rug	$165.00
Ice cream cone	$ 1.50

If you went to work by bus today:
Bus fare — $3.00

Expenses

Plane tickets for weekend trip	$175.00

If you went to work by bus today:
Bus fare — $3.00

Expenses

Box of cereal	$ 2.39
Kitchen chairs	$128.00

If you went to work by bus today:
Bus fare — $3.00

Expenses

New tent	$150.00
Sleeping bag	$ 82.00

If you went to work by bus today:
Bus fare — $3.00

Expenses

Living room chair	$165.00
Picture	$ 45.00

If you went to work by bus today:
Bus fare — $3.00

Expenses

Winter jacket	$ 98.00
Toothpaste	$ 2.29

If you went to work by bus today:
Bus fare — $3.00

Expenses

Television	$235.00

If you went to work by bus today:
Bus fare — $3.00

Expenses

Bicycle	$190.00
Lunch out	$ 5.85

If you went to work by bus today:
Bus fare — $3.00

Expenses

DVD player	$198.00

If you went to work by bus today:
Bus fare — $3.00

(continued)

Daily Expenses with Larger Purchases *(continued)*

Expenses

Eyeglasses	$108.48
Laundry soap	$ 2.45

If you went to work by bus today:
Bus fare — $3.00

Expenses

Special gift for your parents' 25th anniversary	$ 48.75

If you went to work by bus today:
Bus fare — $3.00

Expenses

Camera	$ 55.00
Medicine	$ 33.85

If you went to work by bus today:
Bus fare — $3.00

Expenses

Curtains	$ 52.85

If you went to work by bus today:
Bus fare — $3.00

Expenses

Living room lamp	$ 48.59

If you went to work by bus today:
Bus fare — $3.00

Expenses

Running shoes	$ 55.00
Bagel	$ 1.50

If you went to work by bus today:
Bus fare — $3.00

Expenses

Rollerblades	$ 39.72

If you went to work by bus today:
Bus fare — $3.00

Expenses

Watch	$ 64.98
Newspaper	$ .75

If you went to work by bus today:
Bus fare — $3.00

Expenses

Sheets & bedspread	$ 54.21

If you went to work by bus today:
Bus fare — $3.00

Expenses

Fishing pole	$ 42.69

If you went to work by bus today:
Bus fare — $3.00

Student page 82

31. Paying After You Charge

Here are two monthly credit-card statements. Look them over. Then answer the questions on the next page.

Credit-Card Monthly Statement		June 25
Payment Due Date: July 20		Credit Line: $1,000
Date of Transaction	**Description of Purchase**	**Amount of Transaction**
06/02	Shirt	$ 15.25
06/18	Television	289.43
	Previous Balance	
	– Payments	
	+ Finance Charge	
	+ New Purchases	$ 304.68
	= New Balance	$ 304.68
	Minimum Payment Due	$ 10.00
	Subject to Finance Charge	
	Monthly Periodic Rate	1.5%
	Annual Percentage Rate	18.0%

Credit-Card Monthly Statement		July 25
Payment Due Date: August 20		Credit Line: $1,000
Date of Transaction	**Description of Purchase**	**Amount of Transaction**
	Previous Balance	$ 304.68
	– Payments	10.00
	+ Finance Charge	4.42
	+ New Purchases	
	= New Balance	$ 299.10
	Minimum Payment Due	$ 10.00
	Subject to Finance Charge	$ 294.68
	Monthly Periodic Rate	1.5%
	Annual Percentage Rate	18.0%

(continued)

Student page 83

31. Paying After You Charge *(continued)*

1. What was the total of credit-card purchases in June? $304.68
2. Look at the July statement. How much had been paid? $ 10.–
3. What was the balance that was subject to a finance charge? $294.68
4. How much interest was charged? $ 4.42
5. What is the new balance due by August 20? $299.10
6. Make out the monthly statement for the next month.
   (a) Show blue jeans purchased for $24.00 on August 11.
   (b) Show a CD purchased on August 15 for $15.95.
   (c) Bring the "balance due" forward from July's bill ($299.10).
   (d) Enter a payment of $100.
   (e) Show the amount subject to a finance charge. That's the previous balance minus the payment.
   (f) Figure the finance charge. To do that, multiply the amount subject to the charge by 1.5% (.015).
   (g) Add the new purchases.
   (h) Enter the new balance. (New balance = old balance – payment + finance charge + new purchases.)

Credit-Card Monthly Statement		August 25
Payment Due Date: September 20		Credit Line: $1,000
Date of Transaction	**Description of Purchase**	**Amount of Transaction**
Aug 11	Blue Jeans	$ 24.–
Aug 15	CD	15.95
	Previous Balance	$299.10
	– Payments	$100.–
	+ Finance Charge	2.99
	+ New Purchases	39.95
	= New Balance	$242.04
	Minimum Payment Due	
	Subject to Finance Charge	$199.10
	Monthly Periodic Rate	1.5%
	Annual Percentage Rate	18.0%

7. Which was less, the July bill or the August bill? August
   How much less? $57.06

Student page 84

Answers will vary

See teacher book page 122

Student page 85

Sample

33. Week 8—Living on Your Own

Your Paycheck

Make out the paycheck from your employer for your seventh week of work.

CHECK NO. 07

Nov. 14 20 01 71-587/749

PAY TO THE ORDER OF Lee West $ 225.–

Two hundred twenty-five and 00/100 DOLLARS

FIRST NATIONAL BANK

MEMO

Shawn Ducharme

⑆074905872⑆ 251⑈372⑈8⑈ 4311

Your Check Register

(a) Bring your checkbook balance forward from last week. (See Activity 30.)
(b) How much will you put in your savings account? 6 How much will you keep for out-of-pocket expenses? 75 Deposit the rest in your checking account.

RECORD ALL CHARGES OR CREDITS THAT AFFECT YOUR ACCOUNT

NUMBER	DATE	DESCRIPTION OF TRANSACTION	PAYMENT/DEBIT (–)	√ T	FEE (IF ANY)	DEPOSIT/CREDIT (+)	BALANCE $
		Balance Forward					362 24
	Nov 14	Deposit				144 –	506 24

(continued)

Student page 86

Sample **33. Week 8—Living on Your Own** *(continued)*

Your Savings Account

(a) Bring your savings account balance forward from last week. (See Activity 30.)
(b) Write today's date.
(c) Make your deposit.
(d) Write the new balance.

Date	Withdrawal	Deposit	Interest	Balance
				80.27
Nov 14		6.—		86.27

Your Time Card

Fill out a time card for your eighth week of work.

Employee: Lee West

Day	Hours
Monday	
Tuesday	8
Wednesday	8
Thursday	8
Friday	8
Saturday	8
Sunday	
TOTAL:	40

(continued)

Student page 87

Sample **33. Week 8—Living on Your Own** *(continued)*

Your Out-of-Pocket Expenses

Keep track of your money and how you spend it. If you have large purchases, you can pay by check or charge them.

Cash balance at end of last week (see Activity 30) $ 11.01

Cash from this week's paycheck $ 75.—

Total cash on hand: $ 86.01

Monday Expenses

Groceries	36.34

Cash remaining: $ 49.67

Tuesday Expenses

Bus fare	3.00
Mail package	2.43
Lunch	4.75

Cash remaining: $ 39.49

Wednesday Expenses

Bus fare	3.00
Television (charge)	

Cash remaining: $ 36.49

Thursday Expenses

Bus fare	3.00
Window cleaner	2.43
Paper towels	.89

Cash remaining: $ 30.17

(continued)

Student page 88

Sample **33. Week 8—Living on Your Own** *(continued)*

Friday Expenses

Bus fare	3.00
Saw	14.10

Cash remaining: $ 13.07

Saturday Expenses

Bus fare	3.00

Cash remaining: $ 10.07

Sunday Expenses

Paper	.50
Video rental	3.—

Cash remaining: $ 6.57

Your Charge Account

Purchases over $10 can be charged.

For each item you decide to charge, write the date, what you purchased, and the cost.

Date	Description of Purchase	Amount
Nov. 18	Television	$ 235.—

(continued)

Student page 89

Sample **33. Week 8—Living on Your Own** *(continued)*

Your Checking Account *Lee West did not write any checks this week.*

Use the checks below and on the next page as you need them. What checks will you write this week?

(a) If you pay rent weekly, write that check.
(b) You might want to use a check instead of cash for groceries or other expensive items.

Be sure to record each check in your check register. There may be more checks than you need. If you need more checks, they are on the next page and at the back of the book.

CHECK NO. ______

______ 20___ 71-587/749

PAY TO THE ORDER OF ______ $ ______

______ DOLLARS

FIRST NATIONAL BANK

MEMO ______

⑆074905872⑆ 251⑈372⑈8⑈ 4311

CHECK NO. ______

______ 20___ 71-587/749

PAY TO THE ORDER OF ______ $ ______

______ DOLLARS

FIRST NATIONAL BANK

MEMO ______

⑆074905872⑆ 251⑈372⑈8⑈ 4311

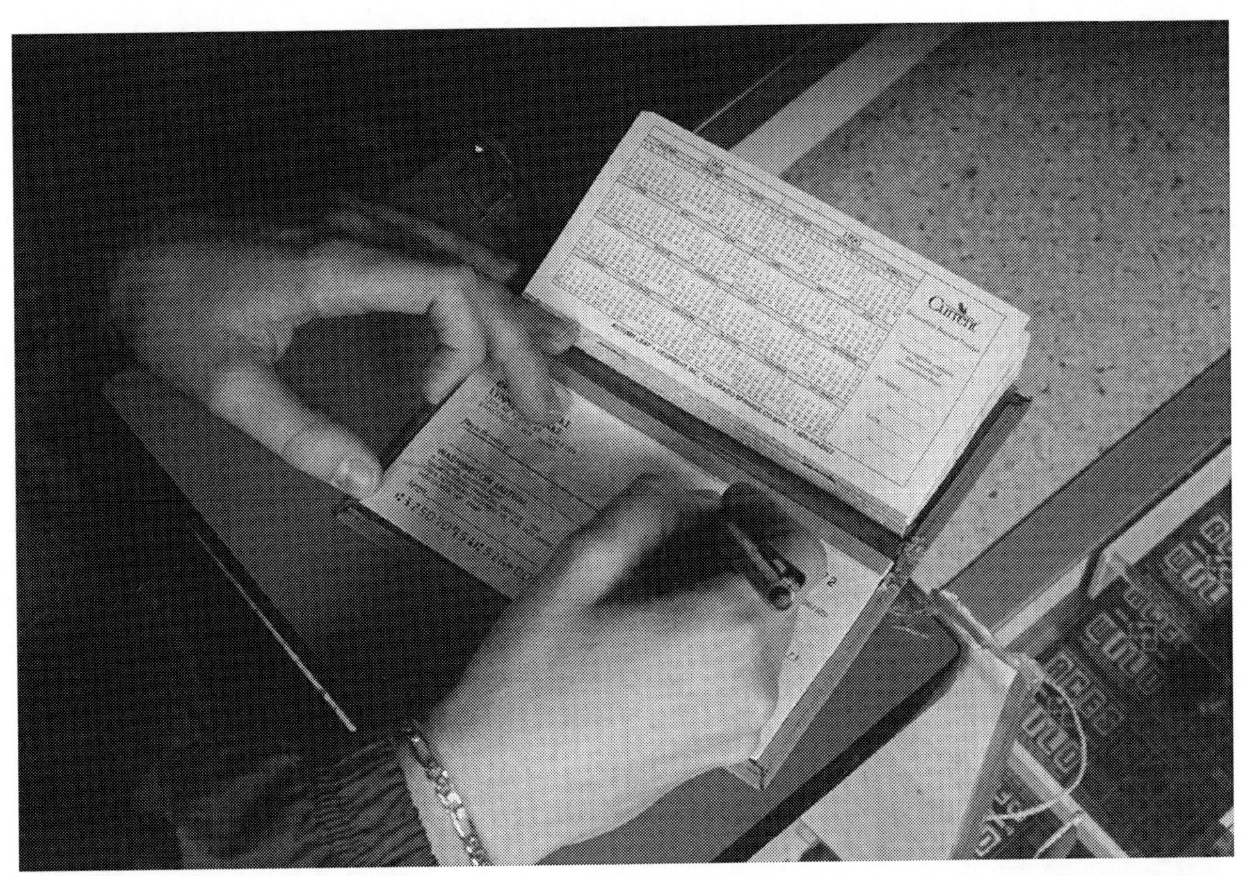

Part 10: Continuing On

Part 10: Continuing On

Objectives

- Students will complete four additional weeks of the simulation.
- Students will review their expenses during the simulation to adjust their budgets.
- Students will review what they have learned during the simulation.

Materials Needed

Copies of Ups and Downs of Life (teacher book pages 133–137)

A box (in addition to the one used for Daily Expenses)

Activity 34: Week 9—Living on Your Own

Copies of the Telephone Bills on pages 138–142 of the teacher book

Activity 35: Week 10—Living on Your Own

Activity 36: Week 11—Living on Your Own

Activity 37: Week 12—Living on Your Own

Activity 38: Adjust Your Budget

Activity 39: Evaluation

Pre-teaching

Little new vocabulary is introduced in these final weeks. But continue to review any words and terms that have challenged students in earlier weeks.

Review vocabulary related to the Ups and Downs of Life when introducing the slips designed for weekly use beginning in week 9. Challenging words and terms include: *funeral, borrow, fee, bonus, oversleep, contest, dentist,* and *pharmacy.*

Commentary: Introduction

Events have been quite predictable so far in this simulation. You have worked to earn a paycheck and then you have spent it. But life is not always like that. Things happen to shake up the normal flow of activities. Some things are good and some things are not so good. As you continue this simulation, you will experience some of the ups and downs of life.

Commentary: Activity 34: Week 9—Living on Your Own

The Ups and Downs of Life that you may face in this unit are printed on slips of paper. You will draw one slip of paper for each remaining week in the simulation. Many of the papers say "normal week." If you select one of these, simply write "normal week" on the line at the top of the first page in Activity 34 and continue as usual. Other Ups and Downs may cause you to lose work or to check your benefits. Do what is written on the piece of paper you draw. You will want to select your Ups and Downs piece of paper before you do much of your week's work. It will not affect your paycheck because your paycheck is based on the work you did last week. But the paper you draw certainly could affect your work or your money handling for this week and for the future.

Note: There are forty different slips of paper included in the Ups and Downs of Life. Fifteen of them say "normal week." It is possible (although not likely) for a student to go through the rest of the simulation with normal weeks. More likely, each student will draw one or two of the variations during the next few weeks of the simulation. If a student happens to select the same slip more than once, you may choose to have him or her draw again.

During this week, you will have to pay your rent—whether it is due monthly or weekly. In addition, during the ninth week of the simulation, you will:

- Collect your paycheck.
- Make a deposit in your checking account.
- Make a deposit in your savings account.
- Fill out your time card.
- Keep track of your out-of-pocket expenses.
- Write checks as you need them.
- Charge larger purchases as you wish.

Activity 35: Week 10—Living on Your Own

Note: Week 10 of the simulation is similar to week 9. This week some students will have to pay utility bills. The amounts of these bills are shown on the apartment descriptions that students attached to the inside front covers of their books. The only exception is the telephone bill. Make copies of the bills in the teacher book (pages 138–142). Give a bill selected at random to each student who has a telephone.

Students will also get interest in their savings accounts. Bring the balance forward from last week and multiply by .004 to find the interest to be added to the account.

Note: The Lee West example shown for week 10 involves rounding a number to the nearest whole cent. Students may need help with this concept when they do their own calculations.

Commentary: Activity 36: Week 11—Living on Your Own

Week 11 is similar to the last few weeks of the simulation. The major difference is that it is time to pay for whatever you have been charging. Add up any items you have charged during weeks 8, 9, and 10 and this week. If you pay the total amount now, you will not have to pay interest. You don't have to pay the total, but you do need to pay at least $10. If a balance remains, there will be interest added in the future.

Commentary: Activity 37: Week 12—Living on Your Own

This is the final week of the simulation. If you did not pay your entire charge bill last time, there will be interest added. Subtract the amount of your payment from the balance that was due. What is left is the amount on which you will be given a finance charge. Multiply by .015 to find the amount of the interest.

Commentary: Activity 38: Adjust Your Budget

Remember the budget that you worked out early in this simulation? It is in Activity 9. At that point, you did not have a very good idea what your expenses were going to be. This would be a good time to look at how you have been spending your money and adjust your budget to some more realistic figures.

Look at your expenses during weeks 9, 10, 11, and 12 of the simulation (Activities 34, 35, 36, and 37). How did you spend your money? Find a weekly average of how much money you spent in each category. Does the total of the averages come within your weekly income? If you were to continue, how would you change the way you are spending your money?

Commentary: Activity 39: Evaluation

Let's take a little while to review what everyone did during this time of *Living on Your Own* and see what we learned from the experience. Answer the questions in Activity 39: Evaluation. Then we will compare experiences and discuss what happened.

Commentary: Discussion Questions

During the first few weeks of the simulation, you made choices: what job to get; where to live; who to live with. If you did this again, would you make the same choices? Why or why not?

You did not have control over your expenses; you drew them randomly. If you had been able to make the choices, what would you have done differently?

How did you handle your finances? With all your bills paid, did you still have money in your savings account and checking account? Did anyone spend more than he or she made?

What have you learned from this experience that will make a difference when you are living on your own? What kind of job will you look for? What type of living arrangement would you prefer? How will you handle your money?

Evaluation

Check student progress and understanding each week by reviewing completed workbook pages. Ask questions like these, using some to help students understand how they can apply their developing skills to their own lives.

- Are the Ups and Downs of Life reasonable? Do things like those happen to most people?
- How can you protect yourself against the Downs of Life? (*Insurance and savings can help.*)
- Have you charged a lot of large items in this simulation? Is this a good idea? What will happen to people who keep building up large charge bills?
- Are the phone bills in the simulation realistic? How can you keep long-distance charges low? (*Shop around for good calling rates. Use e-mail or regular mail instead of phones. Keep calls short.*)
- What kinds of expenses are not covered in this simulation? (*Vacations, hobbies, education, and more.*)

Extension Activities

Talk about the idea of "living on your own." Do most people really try to exist without any help at all from others? Whom can people usually rely on for help even when they live on their own?

Let student questions and interest lead the way to discussion and exploration of other subjects connected with living on your own. Consider asking outside experts to visit and talk with the class about various facets of independence. Or ask students to research some topics and questions and report back to the class. Here are some subjects that might interest students who are thinking about living on their own:

- Health care
  having insurance
  caring for oneself when sick
  reading labels on medicines
  missing work because of illness
  getting dental and medical checkups
- Leisure activities and social life
- Emergency situations
  911
  other emergency numbers
  safety equipment such as smoke detectors
- Citizenship issues
  voting
  getting a Social Security card
  paying taxes
  obeying laws
- Finding out more
  libraries
  community services
  government services
  Internet

Ups and Downs of Life

Photocopy this and the next four pages. Cut apart the slips and put them in a separate box (not with the Daily Expenses). For weeks 9, 10, 11, and 12 of the simulation, have each student draw one paper from this box and incorporate what it says into activities and calculations.

Ups and Downs

Death in the family

The funeral is Tuesday. Do you usually work Tuesday? If so, you will miss work that day this week. Do not draw a Daily Expenses slip for Tuesday.

Ups and Downs

Normal week

Ups and Downs

It's your birthday!

You receive a check for $25! Put it in your savings account, or put it in your checking account, or add it to the cash you have on hand for out-of-pocket expenses.

Ups and Downs

Normal week

Ups and Downs

The bill came

You ordered a magazine last month and the bill came. Make out a check for $9.98 to World Magazine Company.

Ups and Downs

Sick with the flu

You are sick on Friday and Saturday. If you usually work those days, you will miss work this week. You will be paid for sick days. No Daily Expenses for these days—you are too sick to get out of bed!

Ups and Downs

Normal week

Ups and Downs

It's a holiday

Monday is a holiday and you do not have to work. Do you get holiday pay? If so, you will be paid for this day. If not, you will lose some pay. Next week subtract pay for the number of hours you usually work on Monday.

(continued)

Ups and Downs

Normal week

Ups and Downs

Loan to a friend

A friend asks to borrow $10. Put this amount down as one of your out-of-pocket expenses on Friday this week.

Ups and Downs

Clothing ruined

You ruined a shirt and slacks in the dryer. You replace them at Smith's Clothing. The cost is $38.29.

Ups and Downs

Doctor's appointment

The fee for the doctor is $50. Do you have health insurance at work? If you do, there is a reduced charge. Make out a check to Dr. Miles for $10. If you do not have insurance, make out the check for $50.

Ups and Downs

Bonus at work

Your boss rewards you with a $75 bonus at work. Add this amount to your paycheck next week.

Ups and Downs

Normal week

Ups and Downs

Normal week

Ups and Downs

Help a friend move

You help a friend move and are paid $20. Put the money in your savings account, or put it in your checking account, or add it to the cash you have for out-of-pocket expenses.

(continued)

Ups and Downs

Power outage

Milk and cottage cheese spoil in the refrigerator. Buy more at a cost of $5.27.

Ups and Downs

It's Thanksgiving

The holiday is Thursday and you do not have to work. If you get holiday pay, you will be paid anyway. If not, you will lose some pay. Next week subtract pay for the number of hours you usually work on Thursday.

Ups and Downs

Normal week

Ups and Downs

Lose job

You cannot continue your job. You will be paid through the week. But next week you will have to start a new job. Go back to the classifieds to find new work. Ask for a new job description to use next week.

Ups and Downs

Normal week

Ups and Downs

Find money

Putting on an old coat, you find $10 in the pocket. Put it in your savings account, or put it in your checking account, or add it to the cash you have for out-of-pocket expenses.

Ups and Downs

Oversleep

You oversleep and are two hours late for your first day of work this week. For next week's paycheck, you will have to subtract pay for two hours of missed work.

Ups and Downs

Normal week

(continued)

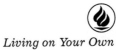

Ups and Downs

Win contest

You win a radio contest and receive $25. Put the money in your savings account, or put it in your checking account, or add it to the cash you have for out-of-pocket expenses.

Ups and Downs

Normal week

Ups and Downs

Normal week

Ups and Downs

Dentist appointment

The fee for the dentist is $65. Do you have dental insurance at work? If you do, there is no charge. If you do not, you will have to make out a check to Dr. Haynes for $65.

Ups and Downs

Loan returned

A friend returns the $15 you loaned him weeks ago. Put the money in your savings account, or put it in your checking account, or add it to the cash you have for out-of-pocket expenses.

Ups and Downs

Normal week

Ups and Downs

Overpayment

You overpaid one of your bills last month. A refund check arrives for $10. Put the money in your checking account, or put it in your savings account, or add it to the cash you have for out-of-pocket expenses.

Ups and Downs

Sick friend

You visit your friend in the hospital and take flowers, which cost $10. This is part of your out-of-pocket expenses for Wednesday this week.

(continued)

Ups and Downs

Normal week

Ups and Downs

Paid for cat care

You care for a neighbor's cat while she is away and you receive $10. Put the money in your savings account, or put it in your checking account, or add it to the cash you have for out-of-pocket expenses.

Ups and Downs

Find money

Walking to the park, you find $10 on the sidewalk. Add this money to the cash you have for out-of-pocket expenses.

Ups and Downs

A friend's birthday

Buy a birthday gift for your friend. You spend $12 at May's Department Store.

Ups and Downs

Normal week

Ups and Downs

Call the glass company

A window gets broken in your apartment and you have to pay for the repair. Make out a check to Rivertown Glass for $23.

Ups and Downs

Medical prescription

You fill a prescription that costs $26. Do you have health insurance at work? If you do, there is no charge. If you don't, make out a $26 check to Don's Pharmacy.

Ups and Downs

Normal week

Telephone Bills

Photocopy this and the next four pages. Cut apart the bills. Each student who has a phone will draw a phone bill to pay in week 10 of *Living on Your Own*.

The Bells Company

Bill for Telephone Service

Basic monthly rate	$ 15.50
Long-distance calls	$ 4.85
TOTAL DUE	$ 20.35

The Bells Company

Bill for Telephone Service

Basic monthly rate	$ 15.50
Long-distance calls	$ 5.15
TOTAL DUE	$ 20.65

The Bells Company

Bill for Telephone Service

Basic monthly rate	$ 15.50
Long-distance calls	$ 8.00
TOTAL DUE	$ 23.50

The Bells Company

Bill for Telephone Service

Basic monthly rate	$ 15.50
Long-distance calls	$ 2.05
TOTAL DUE	$ 17.55

The Bells Company

Bill for Telephone Service

Basic monthly rate	$ 15.50
Long-distance calls	$ 11.95
TOTAL DUE	$ 27.45

The Bells Company

Bill for Telephone Service

Basic monthly rate	$ 15.50
Long-distance calls	$ 6.20
TOTAL DUE	$ 21.70

(continued)

The Bells Company

Bill for Telephone Service

Basic monthly rate	$ 15.50
Long-distance calls	$ 5.80
TOTAL DUE	$ 21.30

The Bells Company

Bill for Telephone Service

Basic monthly rate	$ 15.50
Long-distance calls	$ 11.20
TOTAL DUE	$ 26.70

The Bells Company

Bill for Telephone Service

Basic monthly rate	$ 15.50
Long-distance calls	$ 26.40
TOTAL DUE	$ 41.90

The Bells Company

Bill for Telephone Service

Basic monthly rate	$ 15.50
Long-distance calls	$ 7.10
TOTAL DUE	$ 22.60

The Bells Company

Bill for Telephone Service

Basic monthly rate	$ 15.50
Long-distance calls	$ 8.05
TOTAL DUE	$ 23.55

The Bells Company

Bill for Telephone Service

Basic monthly rate	$ 15.50
Long-distance calls	$ 16.85
TOTAL DUE	$ 32.35

(continued)

The Bells Company

Bill for Telephone Service

Basic monthly rate	$ 15.50
Long-distance calls	$ 7.35
TOTAL DUE	$ 22.85

The Bells Company

Bill for Telephone Service

Basic monthly rate	$ 15.50
Long-distance calls	$ 3.75
TOTAL DUE	$ 19.25

The Bells Company

Bill for Telephone Service

Basic monthly rate	$ 15.50
Long-distance calls	$ 4.90
TOTAL DUE	$ 20.40

The Bells Company

Bill for Telephone Service

Basic monthly rate	$ 15.50
Long-distance calls	$ 8.40
TOTAL DUE	$ 23.90

The Bells Company

Bill for Telephone Service

Basic monthly rate	$ 15.50
Long-distance calls	$ 5.15
TOTAL DUE	$ 20.65

The Bells Company

Bill for Telephone Service

Basic monthly rate	$ 15.50
Long-distance calls	$ 7.95
TOTAL DUE	$ 23.45

(continued)

The Bells Company

Bill for Telephone Service

Basic monthly rate	$ 15.50
Long-distance calls	$ ---
TOTAL DUE	$ 15.50

The Bells Company

Bill for Telephone Service

Basic monthly rate	$ 15.50
Long-distance calls	$ ---
TOTAL DUE	$ 15.50

The Bells Company

Bill for Telephone Service

Basic monthly rate	$ 15.50
Long-distance calls	$ ---
TOTAL DUE	$ 15.50

The Bells Company

Bill for Telephone Service

Basic monthly rate	$ 15.50
Long-distance calls	$ ---
TOTAL DUE	$ 15.50

The Bells Company

Bill for Telephone Service

Basic monthly rate	$ 15.50
Long-distance calls	$ 37.75
TOTAL DUE	$ 53.25

The Bells Company

Bill for Telephone Service

Basic monthly rate	$ 15.50
Long-distance calls	$ 55.40
TOTAL DUE	$ 70.90

(continued)

Telephone Bills *(continued)*

The Bells Company

Bill for Telephone Service

Basic monthly rate	$ 15.50
Long-distance calls	$ 14.65
TOTAL DUE	$ 30.15

The Bells Company

Bill for Telephone Service

Basic monthly rate	$ 15.50
Long-distance calls	$ 9.95
TOTAL DUE	$ 25.45

The Bells Company

Bill for Telephone Service

Basic monthly rate	$ 15.50
Long-distance calls	$ .95
TOTAL DUE	$ 16.45

The Bells Company

Bill for Telephone Service

Basic monthly rate	$ 15.50
Long-distance calls	$ 5.50
TOTAL DUE	$ 21.00

The Bells Company

Bill for Telephone Service

Basic monthly rate	$ 15.50
Long-distance calls	$ 83.45
TOTAL DUE	$ 98.95

The Bells Company

Bill for Telephone Service

Basic monthly rate	$ 15.50
Long-distance calls	$ 6.80
TOTAL DUE	$ 22.30

Student page 92

34. Week 9—Living on Your Own

Sample

Ups and Downs: Death in the family

Your Paycheck

Make out the paycheck from your employer for your eighth week of work.

CHECK NO. 08

Nov. 21 20 01

71-587/749

PAY TO THE ORDER OF Lee West $ 225.—

Two hundred twenty-five and 00/100 DOLLARS

FIRST NATIONAL BANK

MEMO

Shawn Ducharme

⑆074905872⑆ 251⑈372⑈8⑈ 4311

Your Check Register

(a) Bring your checkbook balance forward from last week. (See Activity 33.)
(b) How much will you put in your savings account? 50 How much will you keep for out-of-pocket expenses? 75 Deposit the rest in your checking account.

RECORD ALL CHARGES OR CREDITS THAT AFFECT YOUR ACCOUNT

NUMBER	DATE	DESCRIPTION OF TRANSACTION	PAYMENT/DEBIT (−)	√ T	FEE (IF ANY)	DEPOSIT/CREDIT (+)	BALANCE $
		Balance Forward					506 24
	Nov 21	Deposit				100 —	606 24
6	Nov 22	George Plummer – rent	350 —				256 24
7	Nov 28	The Grocery Store (groceries)	31 92				224 32

(continued)

Student page 93

Sample **34. Week 9—Living on Your Own** *(continued)*

Your Savings Account

(a) Bring your savings account balance forward from last week. (See Activity 33.)
(b) Write today's date.
(c) Make your deposit.
(d) Write the new balance.

Date	Withdrawal	Deposit	Interest	Balance
				86.27
Nov 21		50.—		136.27

Your Time Card

Fill out a time card for your ninth week of work.

Employee: Lee West	
Day	Hours
Monday	
Tuesday	
Wednesday	8
Thursday	8
Friday	8
Saturday	8
Sunday	
TOTAL:	32

(continued)

Student page 94

Sample **34. Week 9—Living on Your Own** *(continued)*

Your Out-of-Pocket Expenses

Keep track of your money and how you spend it. If you have large purchases, you can pay by check or charge them.

Cash balance at end of last week (see Activity 33) $ 6.57

Cash from this week's paycheck $ 75.—

Total cash on hand: $ 81.57

Monday Expenses

Magazine subscription 12.98
Mirror 9.50

Cash remaining: $ 59.09

Tuesday Expenses

None

Cash remaining: $ 59.09

Wednesday Expenses

Bus fare 3.00
Bath robe 24.95

Cash remaining: $ 31.14

Thursday Expenses

Bus fare 3.00
Camera film 6.25
Doughnut .95

Cash remaining: $ 20.94

(continued)

Student page 95

Sample **34. Week 9—Living on Your Own** *(continued)*

Friday Expenses

Bus fare 3.00
Groceries (paid by check)

Cash remaining: $ 17.94

Saturday Expenses

Bus fare 3.00
Birthday card 2.25

Cash remaining: $ 12.69

Sunday Expenses

Toilet paper .89
Dishwashing soap 3.29

Cash remaining: $ 8.51

Your Charge Account

Purchases over $10 can be charged.

For each item you decide to charge, write the date, what you purchased, and the cost.

Date	Description of Purchase	Amount

(continued)

Student page 96

Sample **34. Week 9—Living on Your Own** *(continued)*

Your Checking Account

Use the checks below as you need them. What checks will you write this week?
(a) If you pay rent weekly, write that check.
(b) If you pay rent monthly, write that check.
(c) You might want to use a check instead of cash for groceries or other expensive items.

Be sure to record each check in your check register. There may be more checks than you need. If you need more checks, they are at the back of the book.

CHECK NO. 6
Nov. 22 20 01 71-587/749
PAY TO THE ORDER OF George Plummer $ 350.—
Three hundred fifty and 00/100 DOLLARS
FIRST NATIONAL BANK
MEMO rent Lee West
⑆074905872⑆ 251⑈372⑈8⑈ 4311

CHECK NO. 7
Nov. 28 20 01 71-587/749
PAY TO THE ORDER OF Grocery Store $ 31.92
Thirty-one and 92/100 DOLLARS
FIRST NATIONAL BANK
MEMO groceries Lee West
⑆074905872⑆ 251⑈372⑈8⑈ 4311

Student page 97

Sample **35. Week 10—Living on Your Own**

Ups and Downs: Normal week

Your Paycheck

Make out the paycheck from your employer for your ninth week of work.

CHECK NO. 09
Nov. 28 20 01 71-587/749
PAY TO THE ORDER OF Lee West $ 179.80
One hundred seventy-nine and 80/100 DOLLARS
FIRST NATIONAL BANK
MEMO Shawn Ducharme
⑆074905872⑆ 251⑈372⑈8⑈ 4311

Your Check Register

(a) Bring your checkbook balance forward from last week. (See Activity 34.)
(b) How much will you put in your savings account? 0 How much will you keep for out-of-pocket expenses? 75 Deposit the rest in your checking account.

RECORD ALL CHARGES OR CREDITS THAT AFFECT YOUR ACCOUNT

NUMBER	DATE	DESCRIPTION OF TRANSACTION	PAYMENT/DEBIT (−)	√ T	FEE (IF ANY)	DEPOSIT/CREDIT (+)	BALANCE $
		Balance Forward					224 32
	Nov 28	Deposit				104 80	329 12
8	Nov 22	Power & Light Co.	17 95				311 17
9	Nov 28	The Bells Company	19 70				291 47
10	Nov 28	Smith Oil	13 80				277 67
	Nov 30	Cash Withdrawal	40 —				237 67

(continued)

Student page 98

Sample **35. Week 10—Living on Your Own** *(continued)*

Your Savings Account

(a) Bring your savings account balance forward from last week. (See Activity 34.)
(b) It's time for another interest payment. Write today's date. To find the interest, multiply the balance times .004 (½% monthly interest). Write the amount under "Interest" and add to find the new balance.
(c) Make this week's deposit and find the new balance.

Date	Withdrawal	Deposit	Interest	Balance
				136.27
Nov 28			.55	136.82

Your Time Card

Fill out a time card for your tenth week of work.

Employee: Lee West

Day	Hours
Monday	
Tuesday	8
Wednesday	8
Thursday	8
Friday	8
Saturday	8
Sunday	
TOTAL:	40

(continued)

Student page 99

Sample **35. Week 10—Living on Your Own** *(continued)*

Your Out-of-Pocket Expenses

Keep track of your money and how you spend it. If you have large purchases, you can pay by check or charge them.

Cash balance at end of last week (see Activity 34) $ 8.51

Cash from this week's paycheck $ 75.—

Total cash on hand: $ 83.51

Monday Expenses

Groceries	44.29
Magazine	3.95

Cash remaining: $ 35.27

Tuesday Expenses

Bus fare	3.00
Sandwich	2.75
Soda	.99
Cash withdrawal from checking	+ 40.—

Cash remaining: $ 68.53

Wednesday Expenses

Bus fare	3.00
Winter jacket (charge)	
Toothpaste	2.29

Cash remaining: $ 63.24

Thursday Expenses

Bus fare	3.00
Winter hat & scarf	25.49
Gloves	9.84

Cash remaining: $ 24.91

(continued)

Student page 100

Sample **35. Week 10—Living on Your Own** *(continued)*

Friday Expenses		**Saturday Expenses**	
Bus fare	3.00	Bus fare	3.00
Bucket	7.69		
Sponges	1.68		
Cash remaining: $	12.54	Cash remaining: $	9.54

Sunday Expenses	
Museum admission	5—
Cash remaining: $	4.54

Your Charge Account

Purchases over $10 can be charged.

For each item you decide to charge, write the date, what you purchased, and the cost.

Date	Description of Purchase	Amount
Nov. 29	Winter jacket	$98.—

(continued)

Student page 101

Sample **35. Week 10—Living on Your Own** *(continued)*

Your C

Use

(a)

(b)

(c)

Be

than yo

CHECK NO. 10

Nov. 28 20 01 71-587/749

PAY TO THE ORDER OF Smith Oil $ 13.80

Thirteen and 80/100 DOLLARS

FIRST NATIONAL BANK

MEMO oil bill Lee West

⑆074905872⑆ 251⑈372⑈8⑈ 4311

CHECK NO. 8

Nov. 28 20 01 71-587/749

PAY TO THE ORDER OF The Power & Light Co. $ 17.95

Seventeen and 95/100 DOLLARS

FIRST NATIONAL BANK

MEMO electricity bill Lee West

⑆074905872⑆ 251⑈372⑈8⑈ 4311

CHECK NO. 9

Nov. 28 20 01 71-587/749

PAY TO THE ORDER OF The Bells Company $ 19.70

Nineteen and 70/100 DOLLARS

FIRST NATIONAL BANK

MEMO telephone bill Lee West

⑆074905872⑆ 251⑈372⑈8⑈ 4311

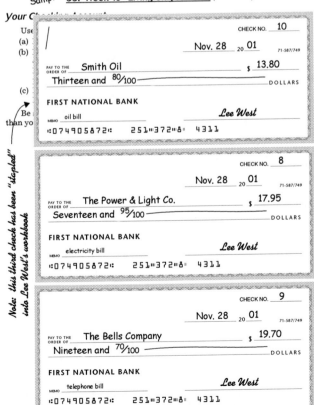

Note: this third check has been "stapled" into Lee West's workbook

Student page 102

Sample **36. Week 11—Living on Your Own**

Ups and Downs: Doctor's appointment

Your Paycheck

Make out the paycheck from your employer for your tenth week of work.

If you missed work or worked overtime last week, look at your job description. It will tell you how to change the check amount.

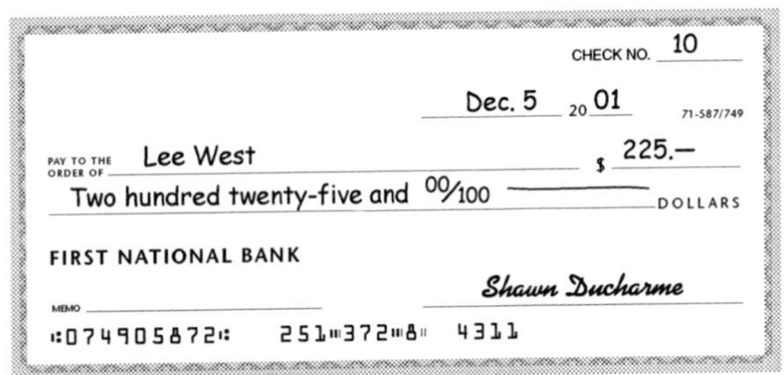

CHECK NO. 10

Dec. 5 20 01 71-587/749

PAY TO THE ORDER OF Lee West $ 225.—

Two hundred twenty-five and 00/100 DOLLARS

FIRST NATIONAL BANK

MEMO Shawn Ducharme

⑆074905872⑆ 251⑈372⑈8⑈ 4311

Your Check Register

(a) Bring your checkbook balance forward from last week. (See Activity 35.)

(b) How much will you put in your savings account? 6 How much will you keep for out-of-pocket expenses? 100 Deposit the rest in your checking account.

RECORD ALL CHARGES OR CREDITS THAT AFFECT YOUR ACCOUNT

NUMBER	DATE	DESCRIPTION OF TRANSACTION	PAYMENT/DEBIT (−)	√ T	FEE (IF ANY)	DEPOSIT/CREDIT (+)	BALANCE $
		Balance Forward					237 67
	Dec 5	Deposit				119 —	356 67
11	Dec 5	Dr. Miles	10 —				346 67
12	Dec 5	The Credit Card	200 —				146 67

(continued)

Student page 103

Sample **36. Week 11—Living on Your Own** *(continued)*

Your Savings Account

(a) Bring your savings account balance forward from last week. (See Activity 35.)

(b) Write today's date.

(c) Make your deposit.

(d) Write the new balance.

Date	Withdrawal	Deposit	Interest	Balance
				136.82
Dec 5		6.—		142.82

Your Time Card

Fill out a time card for your eleventh week of work.

Employee: Lee West

Day	Hours
Monday	
Tuesday	8
Wednesday	8
Thursday	8
Friday	8
Saturday	8
Sunday	
TOTAL:	40

(continued)

Student page 104

Sample **36. Week 11—Living on Your Own** *(continued)*

Your Out-of-Pocket Expenses

Keep track of your money and how you spend it. If you have large purchases, you can pay by check or charge them.

Cash balance at end of last week (see Activity 35) $ 4.54 Cash from this week's paycheck $ 100.00 Total cash on hand: $ 104.54	**Monday Expenses** No expenses Cash remaining: $ 104.54
Tuesday Expenses Bus fare 3.00 Handkerchiefs 4.25 Cash remaining: $ 97.29	**Wednesday Expenses** Bus fare 3.00 Groceries 36.72 Cash remaining: $ 57.57

Thursday Expenses

Bus fare	3.00
Lunch	5.43
Blue jeans (charge)	
Cash remaining:	$ 49.14

(continued)

Student page 105

Sample **36. Week 11—Living on Your Own** *(continued)*

Friday Expenses Bus fare 3.00 Cash remaining: $ 46.14	**Saturday Expenses** Bus fare 3.00 Groceries 17.15 Cash remaining: $ 25.99

Sunday Expenses

Concert ticket	20.—
Stationery	3.45
Cash remaining:	$ 2.54

Student page 106

Sample **36. Week 11—Living on Your Own** *(continued)*

Your Charge Account

Fill out a statement for the purchases you have made in weeks 8, 9, and 10 (Activities 33, 34, 35).

(a) Enter the items you have purchased in the last three weeks.
(b) Enter this week's purchases.
(c) Add the charges to find your "new balance."

The minimum payment due is $10. Make a check out to The Credit Card.

Credit-Card Monthly Statement		**Week 11**
Payment Due Date: Week 12		**Credit Line: $1,000**
Date of Transaction	**Description of Purchase**	**Amount of Transaction**
Nov. 18	Television	235.—
Nov. 29	Winter jacket	98.—
Dec. 3	Blue jeans	19.35
Previous Balance		
– Payments		
+ Finance Charge		
+ New Purchases		352.35
= New Balance		352.35
Minimum Payment Due		10.—
Subject to Finance Charge		
Monthly Periodic Rate		1.5%
Annual Percentage Rate		18.0%

(continued)

Student page 107

Sample **36. Week 11—Living on Your Own** *(continued)*

Your Checking Account

Use the checks below as you need them. What checks will you write this week?

(a) If you pay rent weekly, write that check.
(b) If you have a balance due on your charge account, make out a check for at least the minimum payment due. Make your check out to The Credit Card.

Be sure to record each check in your check register. There may be more checks than you need. If you need more checks, they are at the back of the book.

CHECK NO. 11
Dec. 5 20 01 71-587/749
PAY TO THE ORDER OF Dr. Miles $ 10.—
Ten and 00/100 DOLLARS
FIRST NATIONAL BANK
MEMO Doctor's Apt. ($20 balance paid by insurance) *Lee West*
⑆074905872⑆ 251⑈372⑈8⑈ 4311

CHECK NO. 12
Dec. 5 20 01 71-587/749
PAY TO THE ORDER OF The Credit Card $ 200.—
Two hundred and 00/100 DOLLARS
FIRST NATIONAL BANK
MEMO *Lee West*
⑆074905872⑆ 251⑈372⑈8⑈ 4311

(continued)

Student page 108

Sample **37. Week 12—Living on Your Own**

Ups and Downs: Find money in pocket

Your Paycheck

Make out the paycheck from your employer for your eleventh week of work.

If you missed work or worked overtime last week, look at your job description. It will tell you how to change the check amount.

CHECK NO. 11

Dec. 12 20 01 71-587/749

PAY TO THE ORDER OF Lee West $ 225.—

Two hundred twenty-five and 00/100 DOLLARS

FIRST NATIONAL BANK

MEMO Shawn Ducharme

⑆074905872⑆ 251⑈372⑈8⑈ 4311

Your Check Register

(a) Bring your checkbook balance forward from last week. (See Activity 36.)
(b) How much will you put in your savings account? 6 How much will you keep for out-of-pocket expenses? 125 Deposit the rest in your checking account.

RECORD ALL CHARGES OR CREDITS THAT AFFECT YOUR ACCOUNT

NUMBER	DATE	DESCRIPTION OF TRANSACTION	PAYMENT/DEBIT (−)	√ T	FEE (IF ANY)	DEPOSIT/CREDIT (+)	BALANCE $
		Balance Forward					146 67
	Dec 12	Deposit				94 —	240 67
13	Dec 12	The Credit Card	50 —				190 67

(continued)

Student page 109

Sample **37. Week 12—Living on Your Own** *(continued)*

Your Savings Account

(a) Bring your savings account balance forward from last week. (See Activity 36.)
(b) Write today's date.
(c) Make your deposit.
(d) Write the new balance.

Date	Withdrawal	Deposit	Interest	Balance
				142.82
Dec 12		6.—		148.82

Your Time Card

Fill out a time card for your twelfth week of work. If you miss work or work overtime, show it on your time card.

Employee: Lee West

Day	Hours
Monday	
Tuesday	8
Wednesday	8
Thursday	8
Friday	8
Saturday	8
Sunday	
TOTAL:	40

(continued)

Student page 110

Sample **37. Week 12—Living on Your Own** *(continued)*

Your Out-of-Pocket Expenses

Keep track of your money and how you spend it. If you have large purchases, you can pay by check or charge them.

Cash balance at end of last week (see Activity 36) $ 2.54

Cash from this week's paycheck $ 125.—

Total cash on hand: $ 127.54

Monday Expenses

Money found in pocket	+10.—
Groceries	49.92

Cash remaining: $ 87.62

Tuesday Expenses

Bus fare	3.00
Lunch	6.50

Cash remaining: $ 78.12

Wednesday Expenses

Bus fare	3.00
Lunch	5.41

Cash remaining: $ 69.71

Thursday Expenses

Bus fare	3.00
Candy bar	1.00

Cash remaining: $ 65.71

(continued)

Student page 111

Sample **37. Week 12—Living on Your Own** *(continued)*

Friday Expenses

Bus fare	3.00
Magazine	4.25

Cash remaining: $ 58.46

Saturday Expenses

Bus fare	3.00
Donation to cancer fund	10.00

Cash remaining: $ 45.46

Sunday Expenses

Apple	.50
Band-aids	3.53

Cash remaining: $ 41.43

(continued)

Student page 112

Sample **37. Week 12—Living on Your Own** *(continued)*

Your Charge Account

Fill out your credit-card statement.

(a) What was the balance on your last statement? (See Activity 36.)
(b) What payment did you make?
(c) Did you pay the whole bill? If not, there will be interest charged. How much was not paid? 152.35 Multiply by .015 to find the finance charge.
(d) Record any new charges.
(e) Subtract your payment. Then add the finance charge and new purchases to find the new balance.

The minimum payment due is $10.00. Make a check out to The Credit Card.

Credit-Card Monthly Statement		Week 12
Payment Due Date: Week 13		Credit Line: $1,000
Date of Transaction	Description of Purchase	Amount of Transaction
Previous Balance		352.35
– Payments		200.—
+ Finance Charge		2.29
+ New Purchases		—
= New Balance		154.64
Minimum Payment Due		$ 10.—
Subject to Finance Charge		
Monthly Periodic Rate		1.5%
Annual Percentage Rate		18.0%

(continued)

Student page 113

Sample **37. Week 12—Living on Your Own** *(continued)*

Your Checking Account

Use the checks below as you need them. What checks will you write this week?

(a) If you pay rent weekly, write that check.
(b) If you still owe for charges, you may want to make a payment. Make your check out to The Credit Card.

Be sure to record each check in your check register. There may be more checks than you need. If you need more checks, they are at the back of the book.

CHECK NO. 13

Dec. 12 20 01 71-587/749

PAY TO THE ORDER OF The Credit Card $ 50.—

Fifty and 00/100 DOLLARS

FIRST NATIONAL BANK

MEMO Lee West

⑆074905872⑆ 251⑈372⑈8⑈ 4311

CHECK NO. ____

____ 20 ____ 71-587/749

PAY TO THE ORDER OF ____ $ ____

____ DOLLARS

FIRST NATIONAL BANK

MEMO ____

⑆074905872⑆ 251⑈372⑈8⑈ 4311

Student page 114

Sample **38. Adjust Your Budget**

Look at the budget you proposed in Activity 9. Remember how you thought you might spend your money?

Have your expenses stayed within your budget? To find out, look at how you have spent your money over the last four weeks. Find out how much you spent in categories like housing and food. To find your weekly average, add the amounts, then divide each total by 4.

Item	Week #9	Week #10	Week #11	Week #12	Weekly Average
HOUSING	350.–	19.70 17.95 13.80	–	–	100.36
FOOD	31.92 .95	44.29 2.75 .99	36.72 5.43 17.15	.50 1.00 49.92 5.41 6.50	50.88
TRANSPORTATION	12.–	15.00	15.00	15.00	14.25
CLOTHES	24.95	98.– 25.49 9.84	19.35 4.25	–	45.47
INSURANCE/MEDICAL	–	–	10	–	2.50
SAVINGS	50	–	6	6	15.50
FUN and ENTERTAINMENT	12.98	3.95 5.–	20	4.25	11.55
OTHER	9.50 6.25 2.25 .89 3.29	2.29 7.69 1.68	3.45	10.– 3.53	12.71

Are you living within your weekly income? Should you change the ways you spend money? *Lee West's total of weekly averages is $204.58. His weekly take-home pay is only $225. He will have to make some adjustments.*

Student page 115

Answers will vary

39. Evaluation

1. If you did this again, would you get the same job? ____
   Why or why not? ____
2. If you did this again, would you choose the same place to live? ____
   Why or why not? ____
3. Did you have a roommate? ____ Would you do it the same way again? ____ Why or why not? ____
4. (a) What was the final balance in your checking account? ____
   (b) What was the final balance in your savings account? ____
   (c) What was the final total of your cash on hand? ____
5. (a) Do you have a balance due on your charge account? ____
   If yes, how much? ____
   (b) Have you paid all other bills? ____ If not, how much do you still owe? ____
6. Did unexpected bills upset your plans? ____ If you had full control over your expenses, how would you change your spending? ____
7. List three things you have learned about living on your own.
   1. ____
   2. ____
   3. ____

Extra Checks

CHECK NO. ________

______________ 20____ 71-587/749

PAY TO THE ORDER OF ________________________ $ ________

________________________________ DOLLARS

FIRST NATIONAL BANK

MEMO ________________ ________________

⑆074905872⑆ 251⑈372⑈8⑈ 4311

CHECK NO. ________

______________ 20____ 71-587/749

PAY TO THE ORDER OF ________________________ $ ________

________________________________ DOLLARS

FIRST NATIONAL BANK

MEMO ________________ ________________

⑆074905872⑆ 251⑈372⑈8⑈ 4311

CHECK NO. ________

______________ 20____ 71-587/749

PAY TO THE ORDER OF ________________________ $ ________

________________________________ DOLLARS

FIRST NATIONAL BANK

MEMO ________________ ________________

⑆074905872⑆ 251⑈372⑈8⑈ 4311

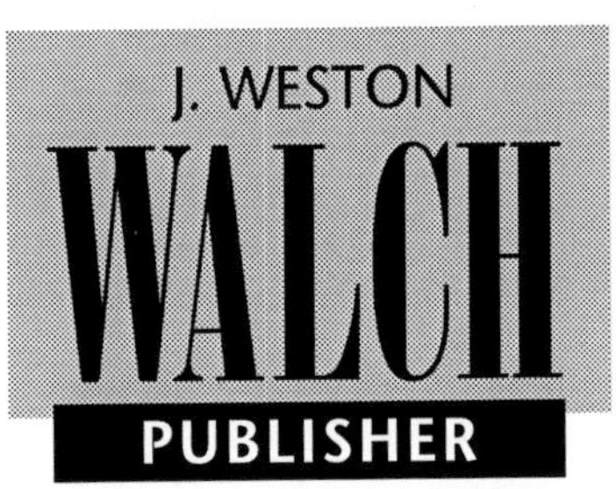

Share Your Bright Ideas with Us!

We want to hear from you! Your valuable comments and suggestions will help us meet your current and future classroom needs.

Your name____Date____________________

School name________________________________Phone__________________________

School address____

Grade level taught________Subject area(s) taught________________________Average class size______

Where did you purchase this publication?____

Was your salesperson knowledgeable about this product? Yes_____ No_____

What monies were used to purchase this product?

___School supplemental budget ___Federal/state funding ___Personal

Please "grade" this Walch publication according to the following criteria:

Quality of service you received when purchasing	A	B	C	D	F
Ease of use	A	B	C	D	F
Quality of content	A	B	C	D	F
Page layout	A	B	C	D	F
Organization of material	A	B	C	D	F
Suitability for grade level	A	B	C	D	F
Instructional value	A	B	C	D	F

COMMENTS:____

What specific supplemental materials would help you meet your current—or future—instructional needs?

Have you used other Walch publications? If so, which ones?________________________________

May we use your comments in upcoming communications? ___Yes ___No

Please **FAX** this completed form to **207-772-3105**, or mail it to:

Product Development, J.Weston Walch, Publisher, P.O. Box 658, Portland, ME 04104-0658

We will send you a **FREE GIFT** as our way of thanking you for your feedback. **THANK YOU!**